I0817350

BLACK PUBLIC JOY

BLACK PUBLIC JOY

No Permit or Permission Required

JAY PITTER

McClelland & Stewart

Hardcover edition published 2026

The authorized representative in the EU for product safety and compliance is Penguin Random House Ireland, Morrison Chambers, 32 Nassau Street, Dublin D02 YH68, Ireland, https://eu-contact.penguin.ie

Library and Archives Canada Cataloguing in Publication

Title: Black public joy / Jay Pitter.
Names: Pitter, Jay, author.
Identifiers: Canadiana (print) 20200396242 | Canadiana (ebook) 20200396307 | ISBN 9780771051913 (hardcover) | ISBN 9780771051920 (EPUB)
Subjects: LCSH: Blacks—North America—Social conditions—21st century. | LCSH: Racism—North America—History—21st century. | LCSH: Anti-racism—North America—History—21st century. | LCSH: North America—Race relations. | LCSH: Black lives matter movement—North America.
Classification: LCC E185.615 .P58 2021 | DDC 305.896/07—dc23

Cover design by Sid Watson
Typeset in Adobe Caslon Pro by Daniella Zanchetta
Printed in Canada

McClelland & Stewart
A division of Penguin Random House Canada
320 Front Street West, Suite 1400
Toronto, Ontario, M5V 3B6, Canada
penguinrandomhouse.ca

1 2 3 4 5 30 29 28 27 26

For my loves, Kirsten Azan (daughter), Greg Jun Guiang (life partner), Ensil Pitter (father), and Esther (dog)

Also, in loving and respectful remembrance of Candida Degala Guiang

CONTENTS

PREFACE

In many ways, this book has been writing itself throughout every Black person's lifetime—a new chapter added whenever we leave our homes to brave and beautifully express ourselves in public spaces. At the same time, the catalyst for this work is a decades-old memory of me swaying to music in a 1970s-style shopping mall and being sharply reprimanded by my mother, who felt that a Black person dancing in public was undignified and reinforced racist stereotypes.

I was maybe eight years old.

Too young to fully understand the implications of her admonishment, I hung my head from the weight of my mother's shame projected onto my lanky little body. All I knew was that she believed that for Black people, especially poor Black people like us, our survival and dignity hinged on *presenting well* in public. Back then, I thought my mother knew everything, so I stopped swaying to the shopping mall music and bore the burden of perfecting all of her public space performance rules.

This book is for her, the little girl who wasn't permitted to sway her body to music in a 1970s-style shopping mall.

–

IN THE SUMMER of 2020, an uprising was ignited by the public execution of George Floyd. Then in my forties, a professional placemaker and adjunct urban planning professor, I had a greater understanding of my mother's, and other Black elders', preoccupation with how their children conducted themselves in public. I was acutely aware of public policies that restricted our public expressions and freedoms, and had witnessed countless incidents demonstrating our disproportionate risks. Within my lifetime, the penalty for a Black person perceived to be misstepping in public had never been more clear than it was in the final, excruciating 9 minutes and 29 seconds of George Floyd's life. I could not bring myself to watch the video but I did not turn away.

I led numerous advocacy initiatives, including writing an open letter to my colleagues titled "A Call to Courage" and hosting online conversations about the broader design interventions and policies that contribute to far too many tragedies similar to the Floyd case. Still, the public conversation, as crucial and catalyzing as it was, felt somewhat wanting.

The notion that Black people should be able to navigate public spaces without being murdered should be a given. Speaking up for this basic spatial entitlement is like advocating for women to be able to freely navigate public spaces without being sexually harassed, or for disabled people to access appropriately designed streets and amenities, or for 2SLGBTQ+ individuals to be able to pee in restrooms of their choice. Many of us would be grateful if these basic rights were a reality. Still, I believe that we should expand our expectations and strive for even more—public joy.

I've led the reimagining of a Confederate monument site in Lexington, Kentucky, integrated women's perspectives in the redesign of a major bridge in Vancouver, developed a cultural district plan for a community displaced by a delayed public transit project, and documented the violence faced by unhoused sex workers in parks. Whether on foot, by bike, plane, or train, I've been on the front lines and experienced how design, policy, and social attitudes shape who gets to experience joy—and where. When leading these and numerous other projects, one of the questions that guides my work is "How can I ignite public joy?"

There is never a simple or consistent answer to this question because each of us has different stories and aspirations which impact how we define public joy. And then, of course, there is the complexity of public places, which, in addition to being shaped by design, are equal parts policy, social attitudes, and alchemy. Most public spaces such as streets, subways, parks, and libraries are technically owned or co-owned by the state, while others such as cafés and bookstores are privately owned. The thing that makes all these places and spaces public is that they are sites outside the home, where our lives collectively unfold.

From Nigerian Igbo markets to Greek agoras, public spaces are fundamentally democratic sites intended to foster citizen participation, prosperity, belonging, and joy. However, they are indelibly marked with historical harms and power imbalances. In this way, public spaces tell us the truth about who we are, and serve as a litmus test for the true state of our democracy and, importantly, our humanity.

–

FOR BLACK PEOPLE ensnared by the transatlantic slave trade, the auction block was their first encounter with public space outside of the African continent. The abuse and sale of these individuals, carried out at everyday sites like courthouses, markets, and plazas, normalized Black suffering and dehumanization in public—a public suffering not unrelated to what the world witnessed as a police officer placed his knee on the neck of a Black man in broad daylight, slowly snuffing out his life without a single individual intervening.

The where of this injustice is as important as the injustice itself.

Despite this brutal history, Black people, even enslaved Black people, have always found ways to cultivate communal and subversive spaces for joy. While shackled to plantations, enslaved Black people started drumming circles, sometimes using their bodies as acoustic instruments. Work songs and spirituals composed in cotton fields lifted their spirits, and at night they used rags and bent twigs as a type of wayfinding through the woods to hush harbours—secret gathering places where enslaved people engaged in restricted spiritual practice. Women wore special headwraps and adorned themselves with handmade beaded necklaces, bracelets, and hair accessories during harvest and carnival celebrations. And some plantations permitted Saturday night dances, where everyone came together to share encouragement, trickster stories, and riddles. Their penchant for joyful community-building continually challenged notions of the enslaved individual staying in their place.

Relatedly, enslaved people participated in lesser-known recreational activities. In his book *Undercurrents of Power*,

Kevin Dawson extols the aquatic culture of both continental Africans and enslaved individuals descended from them. He reminds us that prior to the establishment of the transatlantic slave trade, West Africans were natural swimmers, expert divers, and canoe makers. Due to their proximity to lakes, rivers, and oceans, water was an integral part of their culture, from spiritual practice to rites of passage to daily leisure. These cultural practices and skills were transported to plantations where some enslaved individuals continued to swim for pleasure. Their adeptness in water was so evident that they were considered amphibious and Black women were sometimes referred to as "ebony mermaids." Aquatic acts of public joy enabled moments of bodily agency and respite, and in rare instances, enslaved individuals exchanged their expertise for unique privileges, including wages, and sometimes they quite literally swam to freedom.

Given this history of making magic in the margins, it is unsurprising that Black people continue to play a pivotal role in shaping joyful public spaces. Our sidewalk swagger, front stoop congregations, stylized greeting rituals, and epic park cookouts have not only enabled us to reclaim space, they have granted permission for people of all identities to be their boldest, most audacious selves. Our syncopated rhythm disrupts the street's flow, and like jazz, issues an invitation to collectively improvise. Our urban dialects have created a universal public space syntax constantly translated across cultures. Our expressions of public joy are a type of social capital and infrastructure pushing the bounds of what it means to truly *be* in public.

Yet Black public joy—a joy that the auction block could not extinguish—is often narrowly framed as dope trends or a response to oppression. While both of these are indeed important aspects of Black public joy, this framing is incomplete.

Black public joy is a sophisticated and exciting phenomenon. It is worthy of cultural codification. By this, I mean formally documenting our knowledge, shared values, rituals, and ever-evolving public expressions of joy.

It is not enough to say that joy is already woven into our classic and contemporary texts. There is a difference between creating real or figurative traumascapes with glimmers of joy and laying down joy as a narrative foundation. This is not to deny histories of egregious place-based violation, or the political acuity and galvanizing power of works highlighting these histories. It's to suggest that when joy becomes the premise, the place upon which we build our realities in literature and life, new possibilities within and beyond our communities arise. There is a wealth of documentation focused on our public degradation; why not bend the narrative arc toward Black public joy?

–

AGAIN, WE'VE ALWAYS inhabited public spaces in a bold and joyful manner; however, over the past decade there's been a notable groundswell of Black-led initiatives and expressions. I've delighted in social media posts highlighting Black people fishing, skiing, cycling, birding, and unabashedly frolicking punctuated by hashtags such as #BlackJoy and #BlackOutdoors. And while there isn't always an explicit public space policy or design analysis behind these initiatives, there's a common commitment to celebrating Black peoples' expressions of public joy. These observations and experiences have exposed me to a vibe that transcends conventional urban planning conversations, veering into the poetry of place.

I've met colleagues and community members, some turned beloved friends, who are committed to uplifting the importance of Black public joy within the contexts of urban development and planning, DIY cultural hubs, architecture, and grassroots activism. This aspect of our work isn't commonly discussed alongside critical issues such as the importance of providing housing for those living in parks or mitigating profiling on public transportation. There are no online black square campaigns or pithy protest slogans. However, public space challenges are complex and interrelated. Make no mistake, Black public joy is as urgent as justice.

Together, through the pages of this book, we will journey to places like Tennessee, and the once-bustling grounds of the first "negro" fair, to Detroit, where a historic Black church is being reimagined as a cultural hub baptized "Dreamstead," to Toronto, inside an electrifying, pulse-pumping, world-renowned rave, to Louisville's Jefferson Square Park, beyond the public purview of nationwide protest, and to New York City's badass Brownsville and a rehabilitated track where women are literally running for their lives. These and other narratives are anchored by five parts: Performance, Restriction, Protest, Sacred Space, and Joy, revealing the alchemy and tenets of the book's title. Drawing on my placemaking insights and my path to liberating the little girl disallowed from swaying her body to mall music, I call us all to collective rejoicing—a continual return to the source or place of joy.

PART ONE

PERFORMANCE

I learned to *perform* in public spaces from my mother.

Her public space performance required ritualistic preparation, which began by carefully ironing her outfit, taking a long warm shower, and applying one of those fruity-scented lotions bundled in inexpensive drugstore gift sets. I'd sit on the edge of the bathtub, soaking in my mother's every word as she cautioned me against wearing bright colours and headwraps, pointing to my friends' mothers, who, according to her, lacked proper public space comportment. She'd stress the importance of not speaking in an elevated voice or using large hand gestures in public, and she repeatedly reminded me: "Look everyone squarely in the eye so they don't dare look down on you."

While dusting pastel-pink rouge on her haughtily high cheekbones, naturally sculpted to perfection, she'd explain that Black women must be careful to wear the appropriate amount of makeup, not enough to attract unwanted sexual attention and not so little as to convey a lack of feminine pride. The rules were at once subjective and scientific, the hard line drawn at red lipstick. Red lipstick signalled sexual looseness, which diminished Black women's respectability and safety in public.

Back then, I thought my mother knew everything.

Her beauty evoked awestruck stares from strangers while she waited for the bus or tested the firmness of fruit at the market. At the time I did not understand that her kind of Blackness—light brown skin with loose curly hair—was partially responsible for the treatment we received. Strangers often smiled, sometimes remarking how "exotic" my mother looked, and cashiers politely placed her change in the palm of her hand. She was delighted by this, pointing out how her performance granted us grace and, more importantly, a respect oftentimes denied people who looked like us. My mother believed that Black people's survival and dignity, especially poor Black people like us, hinged on *performing well* in public.

That day at the mall, when my mother demanded that I stop dancing in public and admonished me for perpetuating racist stereotypes, she specifically referenced Bojangles, a character played by Bill Robinson. He ascended to fame throughout the 1920s and '30s, and was one of the first Black actors to appear on major vaudeville and Broadway stages without blackface makeup. Although some applaud him for crossing barbed-wire colour lines, many Black people, like my mother, took issue with his exaggerated facial expressions and movements, and criticized him for "jivin' and entertainin'" in public. She prided herself on her immaculate elocution and never dropped the *g* on her words, so when my mother said "jivin'" with a hard *n*, I knew she meant business.

I've never *not* been aware that my conduct in public directly reflected on my single mother and my entire race. Or at least this is what I was repeatedly told. Heavy stuff for a little person to shoulder. My mother regularly reminded me that being Black, poor, and a girl meant that I would be held to a higher standard of performance in every public sphere of life.

This didn't preclude me from exhibiting what she deemed to be appropriate childlike behaviours in public. My mother beamed when I read complicated words in subway ads aloud and confidently chatted with adults sitting adjacent to us. I was also permitted to carefully kneel on my seat to get a good look out the window, and she happily indulged my many questions about urban landmarks. I was free to express myself and explore public spaces as long as my behaviour didn't breach her exhaustive list of public space performance rules:

- *Never eat on public transit or while walking down the street.*
- *Never wear bright-coloured jeans or lipstick.*

- *Never wear close-fitting clothing, especially if you are curvy or fuller-figured.*
- *Never sing or dance in public, in a mall, or even for Caribana.*
- *Never wear wrinkled clothing in public.*
- *Never look down or avoid eye contact with anyone, regardless of age, race, or social status.*
- *Never wear ripped jeans in public, even so-called stylish ripped jeans.*
- *Never be loud or use "improper" English in public.*
- *Never wear a headwrap over curlers in public.*
- *Never commit a crime that leads to the police knocking on the front door for neighbours to see.*
- *Never sit on the floor at the mall or on a subway platform.*
- *Never idly "hang out" in public.*
- *Never tell private family business in public.*
- *Never respond to male attention in public.*
- *Never enter other people's personal space in public.*
- *Never appear timid or unsure of yourself in public.*
- *Never behave "ghetto" or "uncouth" in public.*

Every kid is taught how to perform in public. I don't mean staged performances, which generally take place in formal entertainment, cultural, and outdoor venues. Rather, this concept builds on social performance, a theory that uses the formal performance stage as a metaphor for exploring how individual identities, cultural rituals, and interpersonal interactions are expressed in social situations. Public space performance is not necessarily inauthentic or a negative. In fact, it can be self-affirming, creative, and deeply joyful. The problem is that my mother's public space performance rules were especially restrictive and fraught with fear and numerous *-isms*. But at the time, like most young children, I didn't question my mother's *wisdom*.

Also, although complicated and risky to acknowledge, sometimes my mother's obsession with perfect public space performance benefitted me. She always kept a lightweight, cheaply constructed blazer on hand and looked my teachers in the eye like someone who knew how to challenge the system if they dared to lay hands on me or attempted to overlook my academic abilities and relegate me to the track team. This obsession also meant that I always had a good book bag, a good coat, and a good pair of shoes, which isn't the case for many poor kids. Most importantly, my mother never marched down the street brandishing a frying pan when I misbehaved, and she never yelled for me to "get my ashy little behind in the house" after the street lights came on.

Even as a child, I noted how this indeed garnered her, and by extension me, a certain level of respect from my teachers and community members. Or as much respect as could be afforded to a single-parent-led Black family living in public housing in the 1970s and '80s.

As I approached adolescence, my identity remained enmeshed with my mother's. As the youngest, and favourite, of two children, I intuited that my penchant for *appropriate* public performance earned me a special place in her heart—a place that could not be penetrated by anyone, including my older sister. Ironically, despite being commended for her striking beauty, my sister was never seen. Her painfully shy disposition rendered her invisible and unworthy of our mother's training. Even back then, I understood the consequences of not performing well for my mother. Being showered with her adoration and approval meant *almost* everything to me. However, when I became a young adult, I risked it all.

Wearing ripped jeans in public became a regular point of contention. I loved, and still love, the daringness of deconstructed denim contrasted by its sensual, soft, frayed edges. My mother thought ripped jeans were evocative of poverty and unbecoming for a *young lady*. At fifteen, becoming a young *lady* was not my priority. We reached an impasse. On the many days that I wore my favourite pair of ripped jeans, my mother passed me on the street as though she didn't know me, withholding her usual warm greeting and hug.

Being publicly ignored by my mother was devastating, but I refused to give in to her theatre of parental objection. The ripped jeans won out, or, perhaps more accurately, my performance exhaustion won out. I refused to continue acting out my mother's prewritten public space performance script, which rendered both of us unable to simply *be* in public.

-

OVER THE YEARS, I grew obsessed with understanding why my mother was so compelled to perform in public. It contributed to me becoming a placemaker—someone who leads the design, policy, and programming of public spaces—and an adjunct urban planning professor. Simply put, I'm a public space expert and explorer. I'm fascinated by how people claim and cede space in public and how design, history, stories, policies, and social attitudes impact those choices. My ultimate goal is reminding everyone that there is enough space, joy, and justice for all of us.

But there was a time when my public space exploration was strictly personal. In speaking with a diverse range of Black friends, I've learned that they, too, were raised with similar public space performance rules and warnings about the fate of Black people who publicly misstep. Almost all of us were discouraged from exploring public spaces and cautioned about the severe consequences of any conduct deemed improper by people outside our communities. My Black male friends were warned about how their very presence in public was perceived as a threat, which, ironically, threatened their lives. We were all lectured about the importance of always presenting extra neat and clean, which for some of us girls ruled out activities like fort-building and swimming that could result in scraped knees or fly-away kinky hair.

Many of us recall watching the news with parents—Sunday sermon saints and Saturday night partygoing sinners alike—who, when the broadcaster announced a crime, loudly prayed the perpetrator wasn't Black. We bore the weight of a stranger's actions—whether shooting up a basement party or stealing a few pounds of steak—on the subway, at the playground, and in workplaces for days following incidents that had absolutely nothing to do with us.

Reminiscing about these and other experiences with our elders, we often dismissed them as hilarious—which tends to be a cultural coping mechanism for navigating difficult experiences within Black communities—or, conversely, labelled them as expressions of internalized racism and respectability politics. While the latter judgment carried some degree of truth, like most judgments, it lacked nuance and grace.

As I've grown, in years and hopefully in grace, I've come to less binary conclusions. It isn't that Black elders thought that perfect public space performance was guaranteed to save a single Black life or were unaware that their rules burdened Black children. To the contrary, Black elders across all social strata understood what Brandon R. Davis writes: "The Black body is never individual, but rather, representative of the Black collective." And many of them would argue that their public space performance rules, deemed harsh by their children and cultural outsiders alike, are far more merciful than the penalty for a young Black person, or community, caught under- or misperforming in public. The irrefutability of these facts is what should be interrogated, not the fear-filled responses of our mothers.

This realization helped me to reconcile that, despite moving through the world with what appeared to be unabashed self-assuredness, my mother was weighed down by invisible yet ever-present public space performance pressure. I was prompted to find a name for the pressure rather than mercilessly critique my mother's behaviour. Every performer has an audience who has the power to praise or rebuke their performance, so I wondered: who was my mother performing for and exactly what power did they wield over her? I shifted from questioning my mother's obsession with public space performance to questioning systems and social attitudes. This new, expanded inquiry pointed me to the gaze.

To be under the gaze is pretty much as it sounds. It is to have an awareness, which is sometimes anxious, of being looked at and judged by other individuals or groups. According to psychoanalytic theory, this awareness can lead to a person losing autonomy by being rendered a visible object. The gaze implies a power relationship between the superior "gazer" and the inferior "object" who is forced to perform and practise self-restriction when under surveillance. The moment I came across the notion of the gaze, I began to understand my childhood experiences in new ways. All the years my mother spent imposing public space performance rules on me, there had been a "superior gazer" who followed her, evaluating her every move.

Through the work of acclaimed author Toni Morrison, I learned about the white gaze, which is the misconception by white people that Black life is devoid of meaning and depth without white presence and affirmation. African American philosopher George Yancy defines the white gaze as an objectification of "the Black body as an entity that is to be feared, disciplined, and relegated to those marginalized, imprisoned, and segregated spaces that restrict Black bodies from 'disturbing' the tranquility of white life, white comfort, white embodiment, and white being." He characterized this objectification as a process of marking, racially categorizing, denying, and physically and sexually violating Black bodies. Professor Yancy also noted the uncomfortable contradiction of desire:

"It is that which is to be feared and yet desired, sought out in forbidden white sexual adventures and fantasies."

In my early twenties, I came across the story of a young woman that helped me to better understand these theoretically dense concepts. Her name was Sara Baartman. She is sometimes derogatorily referred to as the "Hottentot Venus." She was a Khoikhoi South African woman born in 1789. Her father, a bushman, was killed while driving cattle, and she spent her youth living on settler farms. When she was twenty-one years old, she met Peter Cesars, a free Black man who convinced her to move to Cape Town, colloquially referred to as the Mother City, shortly after it had come under British rule. The details of her move to the big city are vague. It is unclear whether she accompanied Peter to the city of her own free will, or by force. What we do know is that she couldn't be formally enslaved as a Khoisan woman, but she did domestic work for Peter Cesars and his brother, Hendrik, alongside enslaved Black South Africans.

She had two children, who both died shortly after their births. Her lover, Hendrik van Jong, a poor Dutch soldier, left her and the Cape behind when his regiment relocated. Soon after, she met Alexander Dunlop, a Scottish military surgeon and friend of the Cesars brothers, whose side hustle was showcasing animal specimens. Dunlop invited Baartman to travel to England to be *exhibited*. Some accounts suggest that Sara initially hesitated but, despite not being literate in English and coming from an oral culture, she somehow signed a five-year contract agreeing to travel to London to be exhibited in public for entertainment.

For five years, Londoners paid to touch Sara's clitoris and ample bottom, the object of their contradictory disgust and desire. She played instruments and smoked a pipe on stage. When both the novelty of the show and Dunlop died, Sara travelled to Paris with a man named Henry Taylor, who then sold her to an animal trainer. It is documented that Sara consented to being studied by scientists, which would be plausible if an individual who was Black and a woman had the power to consent to anything back then. In 1815, at the age of twenty-six, Sara died of what was speculated to be an "inflammatory and eruptive disease."

I believe Sara Baartman died of public humiliation.

A public humiliation so ruinous it transcended her death. Georges Cuvier, a renowned French zoologist often referred to as the "founding father of paleontology," made a cast of her body before dissecting it. This man, who once danced with Sara at a party, maybe even leaning in to whisper something suggestive in her ear, preserved her skeleton and pickled her brain and genitals in a jar. The white gaze firmly affixed itself onto Sara, dehumanizing her. Patrons, also complicit in this grotesque gaze, paid to view her body parts at Paris museums until the 1970s. Following Nelson Mandela's release from prison and ascension to the South African presidency in 1994, he petitioned the French government for her body parts. Sara Baartman returned to the place of her birth not after five years, as promised, but almost two hundred years later.

This reprehensible tragedy didn't simply provide me with perspective on what I'd previously considered to be my mother's irrational fear and obsession with public space performance; I became compelled by the notion of the gaze. And not exclusively the white gaze.

Delving more deeply into Sara's story, I also considered the gaze Cesars, the Black South African man who initially encountered her, cast upon her body. Sara was not only a victim of the white gaze; she was also a victim of the male gaze, an idea popularized by Laura Mulvey's widely read essay "Visual Pleasure and Narrative Cinema." Mulvey's argument was simple: Women are objectified in film because heterosexual men control the camera and the film industry itself. When Cesars, a free Black man from the colonial city, first met Sara Baartman, he undoubtedly viewed her through his privileged patriarchal lens. He also held other social locations of power, such as being wealthy and from a city instead of a rural village. I'm not suggesting that Cesars played an equal role in the homicidal objectification of Sara in Europe or that his gaze held similar power to the gazes of his white counterparts. But, despite having the same skin colour as her, he is indeed complicit in the story of Sara's public demise.

When it comes to gazes of any kind, there are few, if any, innocents.

It is rarely acknowledged that Black people, particularly those who fancy themselves upper class, frequently cast multiple gazes on those considered lower class as a way of separating themselves from those engaged in *undesirable* public space performance. Black people like my mother living in working-class or poor contexts do so for the same reasons and, further, as a way of asserting an aspirational world view.

From flashy, extra-loud Black *cousins* with an abiding affection for ostentatious, thick 1980s rope chains to young Black men demonized for wearing baggy pants and hooded sweatshirts to Black queer folks resisting heteronormative dress codes, there are a million ways to catch criticism within our own cultural communities for performing Blackness in public wrong.

–

I GREW UP in a low-income public housing community and have spent my adult life in the middle to upper-middle class.

Having lived across economic classes, I've witnessed the confusion that can be caused by embracing public space performance expressions associated with different class backgrounds. This past spring, my practice hosted a gathering for Mitchell Silver, former New York City Parks Commissioner and renowned urban planner. Mitchell also happens to be a dear friend.

I was uncharacteristically nervous as my guests swept in slightly damp and eager to escape a spring rainfall. The problem was that, although my guests were prompt, the caterer was running behind schedule. When the food finally arrived, I slipped behind the serving counter, washed my hands, and began to preheat the food warmers and help with preparation. The following day, a guest from that gathering wrote a social media post dissecting the ways I'd performed that evening, differentiating my "charm and elegance" when socializing with friends and colleagues, from my support of the caterers behind the counter. The latter behaviour was characterized as, "Jay from the Block."

And while I understand that his statement was not the least bit ill intended, it reinforced how certain public space performance and behaviours are categorized. Just as people make assessments about what city someone hails from based on their accent or way they wear their jeans, the way we perform in public locates us in a particular class.

Why was I not deemed elegant and charming while supporting the caterers with the food preparation? I wanted the individual who inaccurately assessed various parts of my public space performance to know that I learned elegance from neighbours who couldn't afford high fashion and were inspired to cultivate personal style. I wanted him to know that there is no human more charming than a fifteen-year-old boy trying to respectfully get a girl's attention with handwritten hip hop lyrics and an offer to wear his break-dancing jacket when it got chilly on those early September evenings. I wanted him to know that I didn't become a different person when I slipped behind the counter with the caterers. Rolling up my sleeves to help out when required is perhaps the most elegant thing I did that evening; it may in fact be the most elegant thing about me.

While it is laborious to track which parts of my identity and lived experiences inform my public space performance at any given time, I do know that my childhood class identity, along with its correlating public space experiences, plays a significant role in how I'm perceived in the world. There tends to be an emphasis on race, but class is an essential lens for the development of a spatial dialect nuanced enough to explore Black people's public space performances and, importantly, the way they are judged.

Class is a social ordering that largely emerged in the eighteenth century, departing from hierarchies predicated on one's determined proximity to nobility and religious lineage. The concept expanded during the rise of industrialization in urban centres.

Around the same time, we began to recognize the related concept of *productive forces*, a term advanced by philosopher Karl Marx to untangle the unwieldy and inequitable relationship among "land, labour, and capital."

However, neither Marxism nor classical economics—a theory positioning economic markets as self-regulating systems governed by natural laws of production and demand—adequately confronts how the forced acquisition of stolen land and stolen labour of racialized peoples has inscribed public spaces with unspoken class codes. These codes are entrenched in the very foundation of cities, reinforced by design and policies that shape all human interactions. Class is constantly constituted and confirmed by the ways people behave in public. Sure, class is rooted in capital and land-based wealth, but what is class if not a series of grand public performances between powerful gazers and subordinated objects?

On some level, my mother understood how class played out in public spaces. Rather than resisting public space rules defined by those in the upper classes, my mother attempted to decode and mimic them. This is a common survival strategy for many people who come from newcomer, immigrant, racialized, poor, or 2SLGBTQ+ communities. On an intuitive level, and perhaps intellectually, my mother understood that being unable to publicly mimic middle- and upper-class public performance created a series of physical, economic, and social barriers.

Even in rare instances when formerly poor people of any race ascend to the upper class—through marriage, education, crime, or lottery windfall—their inability to publicly mimic the behaviours of the gazer gatekeepers prevents them from ever truly belonging. Many of these individuals are not afforded the full benefits of their new economic status. This isn't strictly because they have the "wrong" skin colour, last names, or childhood postal codes. It's also because they have the wrong wardrobes, wrong laughter levels, and wrong big hand gestures. Without the right public space performance, regardless of race, these bodies continue to be read as out of place.

The conundrum is that constantly mimicking and acquiescing also results in these bodies being read as out of place. The desperate residue of this type of public space performance reinforces their role as the subordinate object beneath the powerful gazer. As a single mother navigating settlement in a new country, and later an educational pathway that enabled her to purchase a home, my mother didn't have the luxury of time to contemplate these ideas, let alone resist their power dynamics. There was an aspiration to carve out a dignified place here, and *perfect* public space performance was a price she was willing to pay.

Like many immigrants who grow up in this country, I questioned not only the price but also the currency for establishing a good place. When I was eight years old, my second-grade-teacher-turned-second-dad exposed me to numerous public spaces. I was the kid who talked in the back of the classroom while the lesson was being taught and he was the teacher who, instead of labelling the behaviour as insolent and writing me off, challenged me. One day, he asked me to share what I was saying with the whole class if I thought it was more important than the lesson, which I perceived to be a genuine invitation. I don't remember what I said, but I do remember his response. Through parted, upturned lips, he nodded his head and agreed that what I said was indeed more important than the lesson.

He moved my desk up to the front of the classroom, right in front of his, and exposed me to books several grades above my reading level. He helped me to publish my first poem in a regional compilation of students' writing. From second grade onwards, I learned how to respectfully listen and I never sat in the back of any teacher's classroom again.

He took me to the opera and together we visited beautiful public squares, which is rare for kids growing up in public housing in the shadows of the city's vibrant civic commons. Most of the people enjoying the public spaces we visited were white and middle class, including my teacher-dad, but I didn't care. I figured they were fortunate I'd arrived.

What made me uncomfortable was the way these people moved through public spaces. Unlike in my neighbourhood, where my friends and neighbours often hustled and continually assessed the safety of our public spaces, these people wandered and paused in delight. While I was too young to articulate what I was experiencing, I noticed that there was an ease of movement, which I later learned was a result of design centred on them. The streets, parks, water features, and cultural spaces primarily reflected British history, aesthetics, and world views. This created comfort and confidence for those connected to that identity and geography.

All people—particularly the displaced Indigenous Peoples of this land, those descended from stolen and enslaved Black people, women whose contributions rarely receive commemoration, and disabled people denied access—should be reflected throughout public spaces. Recognizing these and other excluded groups within public spaces is challenging because a single site has multiple layers of both fraught and beautiful histories, contributions, and cultural meanings.

However, engaging with these complexities is essential to foster a sense of spatial entitlement among everyone.

Spatial entitlement is a term I use to describe how social conditioning and uneven power relations mediate the quality of public space we feel we deserve, the amount of public space we take up, and the way we move through public space.

At an early age, people of all identities receive direct and indirect cues about how much public space they're entitled to. A child who is told that they should be "seen and not heard" or who is constantly shushed in public spaces will likely cultivate less spatial entitlement than a child who is encouraged to express themselves and explore public spaces. These cues resonate throughout our entire lives. For example, many young women are taught to cross their legs when sitting on the bus or in a café, while young men spread out beyond their seats. Women impose curfews on themselves and restrict their public space routes to avoid harassment and gender-based violence, while men tend to explore new routes and stay out late without similar worries. However, going back to the concerns of Black mothers, because Black boys and men are perceived as a threat, they, too, may impose curfews on themselves and restrict their routes to avoid racial profiling, violence, and murder, despite the absence of a gender-based risk.

This latter example of spatial entitlement reveals its complexity, showing how specific parts of our identities dictate the types of spatial entitlement cues we receive and the number and degree of uneven power dynamics we're subjected to. These and other factors inform the amount and types of public joy we feel we deserve. When I was younger, although I hadn't begun to use and define the term *spatial entitlement* in this specific manner, nor did I yet know anything about the gaze, I sensed how both of these concepts impacted the poor Black, Asian, and white kids I grew up with.

As early as first grade, I noticed the ways many teachers and variety store clerks looked down on all of my public housing friends and how this caused my friends to shrink within or avoid certain public spaces. This included white friends from my neighbourhood. When they showed up for picture day in ordinary attire with a Kool-Aid mustache above their lips, or spoke with Canadian East Coast accents, you could feel their more affluent white counterparts, children and adults, cast a piercing gaze on their poor white bodies.

Across the literature exploring the white gaze in relation to Black bodies, themes of disposability recur, and, interestingly, some white people refer to their poor counterparts as *white trash*. This similarity between the perception of Black and poor white bodies, along with my lived experience growing up alongside poor white kids, is why I've never trusted simple identity narratives or liked the term *white trash*. When we break out of convenient arguments and look at the gaze through a lens that also considers class and how we're conditioned to have varying levels of spatial entitlement, we're able to transcend binaries and better locate our shared struggles—and, most importantly, our shared humanity—in public places.

I didn't always relate to the ways my poor white friends performed in public. Some of them yelled "fuck you" to their moms on the playground when frustrated, and when we got older, a bunch of them got caught up in a heavy metal cult rumoured to involve sacrificial violence.

Black people, especially poor Black people, are obsessed with clean presentation. And swearing at an elder would be grounds for a Pentecostal exorcism. Despite these distinctions, and understanding how race interacts with other -isms, what I do know is that people of all identities, confined to the margins of our cities and civic imaginations, often publicly perform in ways that are messy or, conversely, self-conscious and restricted. Regardless of where bodies considered *other* are located on that spectrum, there is no escaping the middle- and affluent-class gaze.

Growing up in my neighbourhood while venturing out to affluent public spaces with my teacher-dad exposed me to an unusually wide swath of public space performances: From avoiding drug dealers draped in glimmering gold as they receded into dark doorways to enduring the overwrought sighs of wealthy women, always "waiting forever" to be seated at the opera. Early on, I got a sense that experiencing vastly different types of public spaces was a mixed bag of burden, privilege, and survival. This knowing created something akin to guilt within my body, but I was too little to untangle such big feelings at the time.

Several years later, while unpacking moving boxes in an average bungalow she eventually saved enough money to co-purchase with my grandmother, my mother, without making eye contact or providing an explanation, instructed me to never speak about having once lived in public housing. She'd also changed her Caribbean-sounding first and middle names to ones that sounded more Eurocentric. When I asked my mother why she chose her second name, Elizabeth, she proudly referenced the queen of England. I wasn't aware of the full implications of a Black woman taking on the name of an imperial figurehead, but it didn't sit well with my budding Black pride and punk rock sensibilities.

Our move coincided with my mother starting a new job at a well-respected teaching hospital and she asked me not to mention that I had an older sister to her new cohort of colleagues, since that would reveal that she'd been a young mother. Later, when she established a smaller group of friendly colleagues,

I was permitted to acknowledge having an older sister but was instructed to lie about her job and say that she was a computer programmer, which was a big deal in the mid-1990s. Despite the little brown bungalow in a brand-new neighbourhood bringing the appearance of middle-class stability, I'd never felt more unanchored and knotted up inside.

I began to understand that in addition to the white gaze, my mother's public space performance rules were dictated by the class gaze. She'd always been uneasy with her lower class status in Canada. She had grown up middle class in the Caribbean and was rendered poor here due to immigration and single parenthood. In Jamaica, my mother was spoiled by the paternal side of her family and attended private school. When she met my father, a builder and designer from an accomplished family, she was also well provided for. Coming to Canada catapulted her into an unexpected class demotion and, perhaps more profoundly, the indignity of the public space judgment that came along with it. Transcending public housing didn't ease my mother's public space performance rules or quell her shame. In some ways, moving into a new neighbourhood and class bracket ignited an even more intense type of performance paranoia.

Despite beginning to develop deeper appreciation for the intricacies of my mother's journey, I could not dispose of the people and places that shaped me. For my mother, our decade-long stay in public housing was a shameful blip in her lived experience; it was the dignity tax she paid to immigrate to Canada. She didn't feel any connection to the community and often insisted that we weren't like *those people*—meaning our neighbours, who struggled to carve out a semblance of a good life in cockroach-infested boxes and neglected public spaces just like we did.

However, the site of her shame was where I learned to skip rocks in the ravine with my friends and pick berries. It was where us kids sat on the curb out front of the Wimpy's and shared a single box of french fries, a simple pastime that taught me the value and joy of sharing under all circumstances. It was where the older girls braided hair on front stoops and at the basketball court. It was where we played tag until the street lights came on. And yes, it is also true that this is where I witnessed an unspeakable number of public safety tragedies, from rumours of rape in the very same ravine where we picked raspberries and skipped rocks to bloodied brawls in the laundry room when someone "hogged the drying machines." It is a neighbourhood where our friend's older sister, caught up in the local under-aged sex trade, was dismembered and left lifeless in a field. Me and my friends were frequently subjected to unspeakable fear and violent behaviours associated with public spaces. Yet, somehow, we held on to each other and public joy.

After my mother graduated from nursing school, I could not turn my back on my neighbourhood. I continued to feel torn between being relieved to escape the safety issues I faced in social housing and mourning our move. I could not comply with her request to raze the landscape of my childhood. I could still feel that place and those people in the marrow of my bones. I realized that to move through the world with some degree of comfort in my own skin, I would have to carve out a rare, perhaps near-impossible pathway, one that would enable me to navigate public spaces with my large gold hoop earrings and the intricacies of my story intact.

This early commitment to myself helped me when I fell in with a group of Black middle-class friends, whom I met in my early twenties. Their cultural map was marked by an intricate web of beautifully designed pedestrian routes leading to tennis courts, music lessons, and extracurricular tutoring programs. Although I'd been exposed to vibrant public spaces with my teacher-dad, I hadn't realized that public spaces weren't weekend destinations or designated for special occasions. The thought that some people had access to clean, safe, and beautiful public spaces all the time seemed radical. I felt exhilarated to be granted entry into their urban universe, which I would soon learn was located on the more powerful side of the gaze.

One time, a group of us girls were at a mall that bordered a public housing community and an affluent neighbourhood. As we shopped for overpriced designer jeans, another group of youth, clearly from the local 'hood, walked by us. They were rolling deep—meaning there was a large group of them—and leaning on each other belly-laughing. They reminded me of the kids I'd grown up with, kids who, in their late teens, were already being murdered at the park and local basketball court. After the group was out of earshot, one of my new friends nodded in their direction and, perhaps forgetting I was present, said, "I hate being in the mall with that *element*." I'd never heard people described as an *element* before, but I knew it was dehumanizing, and I had to speak up.

To this day, I frequently find myself stretched between the class divides. My public space performance—the ease with which I converse at *fancy* receptions, and closet full of crisp grey pencil skirts—frequently causes those around me to forget my class origin or underestimate my public housing kid pride. Because my public space performance doesn't always align with the type of performance associated with formerly poor or poor people, I've been privy to blunt classist comments made by middle-class and affluent gazers of all races.

Their comments are almost always centred on others in any given context, whom they perceive as being too poor, too loud, too street-involved, too sexually expressive, too culturally expressive, too politically expressive, too boldly dressed, or too emotionally raw in public. My uncomfortable proximity to these comments has enabled me to develop a rare capacity to both dodge and disrupt the gaze in real time. While skipping a sip of my red wine, I have consistently put people casting a judgmental gaze all the way back in their place, which is neither above nor beneath others.

I've also noticed the fissures and fixations behind so-called powerful gazers. These individuals tend to play devil's advocate rather than engaging in transparent public debate. They also prefer private and exclusionary spaces over more accessible public spaces. Women gazers rarely fill their appetizer plates even when hungry and frequently upspeak as though perpetually uncertain. All these gazers are so intent on surveilling and excluding others that they themselves miss out on any real public joy. After all, how much satisfaction can they derive from vibrant public spaces when they insist on presiding over rather than participating in them?

I've learned a lot being in proximity to affluent and powerful gazers, primarily within professional contexts. At first glance, the class gaze appears polished and civil, but a lot of miserable individuals lurk beneath its shimmering veneer. They regularly miss out on experiencing a diverse range of people and expressions, two of the many key attributes of public spaces.

Also, they often engage in or wrestle with many of the same things—such as drug use, mental health challenges, and violence—that they condemn. Their access to private spaces such as intergenerational family homes, cottages, yoga retreats, and treatment centres conceals their vulnerabilities, reinforcing their powerful positions. In reality, gazers aren't so much elevated, they are protected and estranged in rarified locations of their own making.

Poor people and those whose struggles are on public display are no better or worse. They simply have fewer private spaces to conceal what may be considered undesirable and complex parts of the human condition. This disproportionately exposes them to external gazes that project judgment and violence onto their bodies in public places. Powerfully presiding over public spaces or self-consciously hyper-performing in public spaces diminishes everyone.

There are few things more cannibalizing than the white gaze on Black and brown bodies, the male gaze on female and gender-nonconforming bodies, the able-bodied gaze on disabled bodies, and the affluent gaze on poor bodies. All of these gnaw at the cartilage and consume the lifeblood of their objects while disconnecting gazers from community and meaningful connection.

In moments when I'm privy to someone casting a gaze on the bodies of others, and when I am unconsciously doing so myself—again, there are no innocents—I strive to remember that we're all navigating systems and physical spaces that undermine the highest expression of harmonious human connection. With this in mind, I began to explore creative ways of subverting the hierarchies, violence, and inhumanity imposed by external gazes.

I came across the concept that the body isn't simply a shell or container, but rather, it is an actual place interacting with other places, both natural and constructed. I found this idea of the *body as place* to be a useful frame for thinking about creative ways of deflecting the gaze and reclaiming and rerooting our public space performance.

Understanding that both interpersonal and structural issues can profoundly pollute the body—metaphorically, physically, and politically—provides a foundation for disrupting multiple types of gazes and hostile cultural cartographies. Just as the body is the referential point from which we establish spatial concepts such as front, back, up, and down, the body is a place that has an internal navigation system that can help us deconstruct the harmful messages projected onto its surface while creating a safe(r) and sacred internal place of self-affirmation.

These ideas bring me back to a photo of my grandmother, now deceased, flanked by her two sisters on a Caribbean beach. All three women, in their late thirties to mid-forties, are wearing brightly coloured swimsuits. My grandmother, the eldest of the sisters, is predictably posing in the middle wearing a mustard-coloured swimsuit, round belly bulging, beaming with pride. Grand Auntie Anita and another sister I never met stand beside her wearing equally bright swimming suits and smiles. Their shoulders are squared off with the camera, not positioned sideways to conceal their bellies or create the illusion of thinner hips. All three women are concurrently occupying both places—their bodies and the beach.

Even as a young girl, I could tell that they all exuded a confidence from within, and although in front of the camera, they weren't particularly posing for the camera. When I assess the photo, I keep in mind that these women were living on their home island, where most people looked like them and where they, as light-complected women, exemplified the beauty standard of the day, at a time before digital platforms tallied likes and comments measuring women's desirability. Still, I'm struck by the culturally distinct way that I've observed them and other Black women occupy their bodies as place across historical and geographical contexts.

Despite being hyper-vigilant about the public space performance of their children and other loved ones, again largely as an expression of care, safety, and social mobility, Black women have also embraced a bold form of public space pageantry. Many Black women across cultures have rejected Western notions of maintaining girl-like bodies well into adulthood or refraining from wearing particular clothing and hairstyles after a certain age. They were ahead of the whole "The beach is going to get the body I give it" movement. Black women like my grandmother were flaunting plump stomachs, hips, and bottoms on beaches and at block parties long before. Heck, some Black women wear halter tops and gold sequined sandals to get a quart of milk at the corner store.

I have never met a human more unapologetically visible and audible in public than a Black woman. Even, and perhaps especially, Black women navigating precarious situations—beneath external gazes, they exhibit unfathomable public space pageantry. The women my mother loathed as loud and distasteful were some of the most vibrant women I'd ever witnessed. Their brightly coloured headwraps, paired with neon-coloured skin-tight jeans, represented a form of pageantry and creative resistance I admired growing up and still admire today.

When thinking about pageantry and creative resistance, the architect and burlesque artist Sapphira Charles comes to mind. "I've always been interested in the ways public expressions of sensuality could contribute to a sense of joy for Black people, women, and queer folks," she says. In high school she designed and constructed a Plexiglas erotic palace for a class assignment. As a young woman growing into her sensuality, she yearned for transparent dialogue about parts of ourselves deemed too dirty for public consumption.

Her exploration of these ideas continued throughout her studies in architecture at both the undergraduate and graduate levels. "In my first-year studio, I made a series of life-sized modular bra cups out of wire and latex, and couldn't have been more pleased when my professors noted the sensuality of the design," she says. After university, she did something that most architects, entrusted with the design of domestic and public spaces, wouldn't dare—she began to dance in burlesque shows.

Covered by a 40-foot skirt constructed from parachute material, Sapphira slowly emerges wearing all-white lingerie with a matching wig, silently wailing to Pink Floyd's "The Great Gig in the Sky." Rising to her knees, then her feet, she invites the audience to explore the contours of her inner thighs and lace-covered breasts through a series of interpretive dance moves. She works her way out of the skirt, which is then transformed into a textile landscape upon which she exposes the body and built environment as places defined by brutal beauty standards and aspirations of the powerful.

The notion of body as place also brings me back to Sara Baartman's story. I recalled that she smoked cigars and played instruments beneath an unspeakably objectifying gaze. Later in her life, in France, when asked to remove all her clothes, she refused. It occurred to me that these actions also exemplified a form of pageantry and creative resistance that disrupted an uncomplicated victim narrative. All of these women—my elders on the beach, women from the public housing community where I grew up, Sapphira Charles, and this young woman whose haunting story has followed me for decades—understood that their bodies were more than possessions or sites for suffering external gazes.

When external gazes attempt to render me an unworthy or alien object out of place, I seek refuge in my body. Instead of internalizing microaggressions, I play prerecorded messages in my body.

If I enter a public place or space and elicit the attention of people who don't look like me, as long as I don't sense an imminent safety risk, I don't waste precious energy parsing out their motivations. Instead, I repeat my healthy spatial entitlement messages. I remind myself that I belong wherever

I am. I belong in public spaces that contribute to my health, opportunity, and sense of curiosity. I then tell myself that I'm attracting so much attention because of my swagger, striking features, fashionable outfit, and/or the vibrant energy I brought into the space.

I joke with friends that these messages I've been telling myself may not be entirely accurate. I'm certain that, on occasion, I have been unwelcome or viewed as performing inappropriately. However, establishing a sense of belonging from the inside out and playing positive prerecorded messages have saved me from expending precious time grappling with the negative perceptions of people who neither know nor value me. In this way, I've used body as place and cultivated my own embodied practice for deflecting the gaze while navigating public spaces. I believe that everyone should have their own healthy spatial entitlement messages ready to repeat when their authentic performance or experiences of public joy are threatened. Doing this has helped me to quickly reclaim the beauty of many moments, which otherwise would have been stolen by directing too much attention to biased and unkind gazes.

In addition to seeking belonging within my body, I've questioned the very concept of belonging. Most of us have the innate yearning to belong, which prolific scholar and activist bell hooks described as firm ground upon which to create, drink tea, and be in fellowship with others.

Like hooks, we should all take a moment to contemplate what belonging means for us and compose our own personal belonging mini-manifestos. Additionally, we should recognize the limitations and dangers of seeking to belong. Childhood cliques teach us a simple lesson about this. Many young people spend hours painstakingly figuring out how to get in with the cool crowd. The social status and powerful gaze of those kids stop them from recognizing that cliques are often cruel and exclusionary. Even as adults, we need to build comfort and resilience with *not* belonging.

Growing comfortable with the uncomfortable feeling of not belonging is liberating and an important part of becoming more of ourselves. In addition to the messages I play when I sense a biased gaze, embracing the discomfort of feeling like I don't quite belong is another one of my embodied strategies for resisting. I firmly believe that it is my democratic and spiritual right to feel a sense of belonging everywhere, and, by extension, I feel that we all have a moral obligation to contribute to one another's sense of belonging. However, public places and spaces that may harm my physical or mental health, or that require me to betray core parts of my identity and values, are simply not worth striving to belong to. Learning to manage my natural human yearning to belong while becoming accustomed to being with myself has been a precious personal growth milestone for me.

When I was approaching my thirtieth birthday, many years ago, I started taking myself on really lovely dinner and movie dates. I was initially self-conscious and extremely focused on the stories people were telling themselves about me being a young woman out *alone*. I often brought a magazine with me and avoided eye contact with others in an attempt to disappear into the backdrop of bustling social landscapes. And then it happened: One day I found myself quietly enjoying my dinner, exploring my own thoughts, and I realized that I *was* out with someone—me. For the first time ever, being out in public with myself was not only enough, it felt delightful.

To some extent, all of us feel the pressure to perform and we frequently betray our bodies as place by becoming fixated on external gazers and expectations set in childhood. It saddens me when I contemplate how much is missed when we're unable to be present in our bodies and in public places because we are so busy performing in ways that diminish our experiences.

Imagine how much is lost from not relaxing our shoulders and lingering long enough to feel, not just hear, the live music emanating from a patio, or not kicking off our shoes in a park to feel the tickle of grass blades between our toes. Imagine the tragedy of not sharing a long embrace at the bus station or weeping at the city's inexplicable melancholy when it rains in autumn. Now imagine how much is missed navigating public spaces in a body which has been placed on an auction block, perceived as a product.

PART TWO

RESTRICTION

In the mid-1700s, a century prior to the end of the American Civil War, runaways and renegades wrote personal accounts predominantly focused on what Henry Watson, an enslaved African American, described as the "language and ceremony" of the slave auction. For Black people ensnared by the transatlantic slave trade, the auction block was their first encounter with public space in these new countries. It induced a terror greater than the cowardly crack of the whip as it marked the beginning of a long walk into an unknown suffering. It's believed that forgotten places and dormant memories can be retrieved and reshaped as current dreams. And so, we find ourselves here, at the auction block, not as a lament or preoccupation with the past but as a way to understand the scrutiny and high stakes of Black people's public space performance.

On the day of the sale, enslaved people of African descent were made to meticulously groom themselves and put on their best clothes as though preparing for a festive occasion.

Sometimes extra grease would be applied to their mouths to make it appear as though they'd just eaten a hearty meat dish, an unusual practice given that everyone knew enslaved individuals rarely ate meat. As buyers and spectators gathered in the public square, the enslaved individuals were warned to swallow fears of being separated from their partners and children, to look lively, and to politely answer questions. Sometimes they were made to sing and dance, an especially cruel absurdity.

However, the most brutal aspect of the auction was the public indignity of the assessment, oftentimes carried out by the city officer. Men, women, and children stood in separate lines whispering prayers to both God and Allah. Everyone's teeth and hands were examined, and special attention was paid to excessive whip marks on the back and limbs, as those were indicative of a fiery, disobedient constitution. Women were fondled openly and sometimes taken to an adjacent room for *further inspection*. Advanced mental capacity was deemed a deficiency. I believe this is because free thought is the precursor to free movement and, by extension, freedom movements. The sustained oppression of a group has historically been contingent on restricting the body, mind, movement—and, most egregiously, the geography of the imagination. This form of violence is not uniquely committed against Black people; what is distinct is the visibility and ordinary nature of the violation.

We've miscalculated the impact that the normalization of the sale of restricted Black bodies had. These violations were not hidden in attics or death camps or at the rural road's end, but carried out in public spaces where decent people fingered textiles and debated politics, and this continues to adversely shape the experiences of Black people today. People casually bought, sold, beat, and sexually violated Black people at everyday sites—in front of courthouses, at the centre of bustling markets, and on well-travelled streets.

The absence of place—meaning our tendency to talk about race and other parts of identities in abstract structural and theoretical terms—leaves us tongue-tied when attempting to confront daily indignities and hatred carried out with impunity in plain view. It distorts the violation itself, giving rise to a powerful form of personal and social dissonance. Take, for instance, my distant cousin Gussie.

Throughout the 1990s, Gussie was employed as a farm worker here in Canada. My grandmother, a complicated but hospitable Pentecostal woman who moved to Canada in the late 1960s, referred to him as "country," alluding to his rural Jamaican roots. She plied him with unsolicited prayers and homemade meals each weekend. Gussie seemed genuinely appreciative of spending time in my family's modest bungalow, a reprieve from the small trailer he shared with four other workers on the farm. I think that having Canadian family members pick him up each weekend made him feel cared for and dulled the sharp edges of loneliness from leaving his family for half the year.

By that time, I'd given birth to my daughter, Kirsten, and my mother had moved out, leaving Kirsten and I with the basement suite of our intergenerational family home while my grandmother and her husband continued to reside on the main floor. Every year before Gussie arrived, my grandmother, referred to as "Mama" by all, warned me to "mek Gussie feel welcomed."

Gussie, who was in his early thirties at the time, had two children of his own, and so, despite having little in common, we found a way to make small talk about our little ones. His hands were perpetually buried in his pockets and his eyes fixed on the floor, two habits I found mildly annoying, but he immediately became enlivened when I broached the topic of farm work. As a city kid, I didn't quite understand his love for working with soil—planting seeds, inspecting crops, and being entrusted with the operation of large machinery—but I respected it. His connection to the earth and the opportunity it created for him to provide for his children "back home" were palpable.

Once, I inquired about how he'd come to work on the farm and was almost undone by his response. He said his employer, a Canadian farmer, travelled to Jamaica and, with the help of a local, had the strongest men assembled in the market square for *inspection*. The men were instructed to remove their shirts, display their backs and arm muscles, open their mouths to have their teeth checked, and hold out their hands for a "roughness test." I'll never forget the proud, slow parting of Gussie's lips as he explained that men with soft hands were immediately dismissed from the lineup because they lacked the physical fortitude for farm work. He was one of the few men left standing, in public, where his neighbours sold fried fish and wood carvings, having been deemed strong stock.

Gussie then held out his calloused hands to me—hands that laboured so his daughters could attend school in crisp, properly fitted uniforms and his wife could watch her soap operas on their very own television. He was proud of being able to provide his family with a level of leisure and education often denied poor country folk. Although I was twenty-something and still in the business of being right about everything, I resisted the urge to tell Gussie that his *interview process* had actually mirrored that of our enslaved ancestors, that he had been both violated and chosen in public. Instead, I silently held his calloused hands in mine.

To this day, I am thankful for the rare wisdom of my youthful silence.

My cousin Gussie's lack of awareness about how the public inspection for his farm work job mirrored the ceremony of the slave auction block an entire century after emancipation is not strictly due to his lack of formal education. Right across North America, there's been an intentional erasure of difficult histories of all kinds from the public realm. Author and scholar Anne C. Bailey, also a Jamaican expat, wrote a brilliant *New York Times* article underscoring the prevalence and impact of this erasure across the United States.

Bailey notes that after the Civil War, the state emphasized reconstruction and national unity to distance itself from its shadowy past. Meanwhile, formerly enslaved African Americans immediately set out to find the very places the state wanted to forget. With little more than hope and personal mementos, they set out to find their loved ones, only to discover that most of the auction blocks had been removed and the auction houses had been repurposed. Many people were eager to erase any living memory of these places.

I'm compelled by this idea of living memory—how taking the time to look back and redress place-based transgressions can help us to create spaces that honour the fullest, most joyful public expression of ourselves. An expression denied Black people, who occupied public spaces as product for more than four hundred years.

This harmed Black people's sense of healthy spatial entitlement and seeded a sense of hyper-vigilance, while indoctrinating non-Black people with fear, suspicion, and a sense of superiority, distorting the ways they view and navigate bodies that look like mine. This is an intertwined pathology—a betrayal of the city's promise of a vibrant shared commons and civil society. By marking auction block sites, we will be able to, as Bailey suggests, create a more "equitable map," and uncover hidden and subversive municipal laws and policies that continue to perpetuate the restriction of Black people's joy in public spaces.

In fact, before the ink on the Emancipation Proclamation dried, declaring "that all persons held as slaves . . . are, and henceforward shall be free," America, and many other slave-holding countries, leveraged numerous public space laws that Katherine McKittrick, an eminent and fierce cultural geography scholar, asserts are "connected to practices of domination and deliberate attempts to destroy a black sense of place." Although the high seasons of "slave catching" and lynching are over, their violent legacies continue through state-sanctioned enforcement of public spaces.

Overall, public spaces are heavily surveilled sites, where bodies deemed out of place or vulnerable in place are controlled by hidden and underexplored laws. Because society has not fully recognized or atoned for the cultural, economic, and spiritual devastation of slavery, there is an unarticulated yet visceral fear that Black bodies—bought, sold, and brutalized in public—will rise up in collective vengeance. This unsubstantiated fear has recast Black people from a victimized group deserving of redress and joy in public spaces like everyone else to a public threat that must be controlled.

From the very moment my ancestors leapt off the auction block, the state has weaponized a series of laws to restrict our movement. It started with laws that permitted the re-enslavement of freed Black people in states like Mississippi, where a "free negro" could be sold back into slavery if they spent more than ten days in the state, and laws that prevented free Black people from entering so-called progressive Northern states. These laws exemplified the fallacy of freedom, perfectly summarized by W.E.B. Du Bois, the distinguished historian and activist, who wrote, "The slave went free; stood a brief moment in the sun; then moved back again toward slavery."

Sundown towns imposed a series of exclusionary housing covenants and used harassment and physical violence to keep Black people, other racialized groups, and Jewish people outside the city limits after sundown. These laws emerged in the late 1800s and continued to expand until the late 1940s. It's been said that around the time of reconstruction, someone in Gardnerville, Nevada, blew a whistle at six o'clock every evening as a warning to Indigenous people to leave town; in Colorado, signs read "No Mexicans After Night"; and Connecticut was a little less direct with "Whites Only Within City Limits After Dark." Due to population size and visibility, intermingled with the bitter aftertaste of the Civil War, Black people were the primary targets of sundown town laws, so much so that police sometimes met Black passengers at train stations to apprise them of the curfew. For additional clarity, signs were posted at the city limits that read "N***** Don't Let the Sun Go Down on You."

When he began his research for his book *Sundown Towns*, James W. Loewen, a foremost expert on this relatively hidden history, thought he'd find ten sundown towns in his home state of Illinois and fifty sundown towns across the U.S. I imagine his disheartenment when he learned there were 507 sundown towns close to home and thousands across the U.S. My own heart sank when I delved beneath the sanitized veneer of Canadian history to discover sundown towns like Leamington and Kingsville in my home province of Ontario.

It is impossible to decouple sundown town laws from Jim Crow laws that mandated racial segregation in public places and spaces like schools, swimming pools, and buses through the legal rhetoric of "separate but equal." These laws worked together, ensuring Black people couldn't reside in, spend significant amounts of time in, or access common public spaces, rendering us free-ish. Essentially, the cartography of the plantation was overlaid on the city long before redlining limited where we could purchase homes.

In 2020, similar curfews were imposed in approximately forty cities and counties during the civil rights uprising precipitated by the roadside public execution of George Floyd, and other fatal incidents of police brutality and structural racism. At that time, which now simultaneously feels like a second and a century ago, activists and journalists critiqued the efficacy of these curfews due to fatalities of both Black and non-Black people, as well as escalating police aggression, but we failed to ask: Why are we still imposing racist, state-sanctioned restrictions that date back to slavery?

I wanted to learn more, so I approached Isaiah Trickey, the son of American civil rights activists and ex-patriots. His mother, Minnijean Brown-Trickey, is an internationally renowned leader who was a member of the Little Rock Nine—a group of nine Black youth who desegregated Arkansas's Little Rock Central High School in 1957 after segregated schools were deemed unconstitutional. His father, Roy Trickey, is the son of a white Presbyterian preacher turned hippie who kept company with Black liberation fighters like Stokely Carmichael, and he later became a scientist.

The couple met at Southern Illinois University, located in a sundown town, so theirs was a literal, not metaphorical, wrong-side-of-the-tracks love story. A Black person like Minnijean could have been shot on sight if she dared to travel to the white side of the train tracks after dark, and Roy would have been deemed a *n***** lover* if he ventured over to the Black side. They decided to live on the white side, where Minnijean, a gifted college student, could be explained away as Roy's domestic worker. Typical of a small town, it didn't take long for their clandestine and illegal living situation to be brought to the attention of the fire chief, who gave them the courtesy of a warning to leave town instead of immediately burning down their house. Soon afterwards, Roy was drafted to fight in the Vietnam War, and when his request to be granted conscientious objector status was denied, the couple fled to Canada, where Isaiah and his siblings grew up and currently live.

Isaiah heard the story of his parents' early romance for the first time a few years ago while driving around that same small town with his father, searching for barbecue and traces of a now-imperceptible history.

Given the race- and place-based complexity of Isaiah's background, I asked him how he identifies. Without pause, he told me: "I have no choice in the matter; history has decided for me. The moment I step outside of my home, I'm identified as a Black man and treated accordingly."

Isaiah recalls growing up anonymously, home-schooled in a Northern Ontario town without a phone or electricity in the 1970s and early 1980s. When he and his siblings were at the park on the street close to their home, local children would call them "n*****." They never told their parents. "It was the seventies; we didn't talk to our parents as equals then, and we didn't really understand who they were, or who we were," he says. "At the time, I didn't know about the racial attacks my mother experienced as a Black youth desegregating her high school in America, and she didn't know that we were experiencing the same racial attacks in a small town across the border . . . the very thing she was trying to protect us from but couldn't."

His words sting the skin on my face like an unexpected January gust.

Isaiah first learned about his mother's experience from a movie script titled *Crisis at Central High*, which had been sent to their home for his mother's review and comments. His sister Morningstar, a few years older with advanced reading skills, caught a glimpse of the script, and as she read its words aloud, both young children realized their mother was at the centre of its plot line. Prior to the film's release, the parents sat their children down and told them about Minnijean's experiences, but it wasn't until Isaiah watched her in *Eyes on the Prize*, a documentary series, several years later that anger and curiosity set in.

On the afternoon that I'm scheduled to speak with Minnijean, I am uncharacteristically nervous. I'm unaffected by celebrity, but this woman is quite literally a hero, and, as someone who has navigated restricted Black spaces in both Canada and America, she is one of the few living authorities able to speak to this issue across borders and time. I'm eager to learn from her experiences and, as taught by my ancestors, including my late grandmother, I humbled myself at the feet of this elder.

When Minnijean answers the phone, I immediately note the rich earthiness of her voice, a quality not unlike Nina Simone's and Maya Angelou's—Black women rarely upspeak as though asking a question or seeking approval—and an authentic warmth cultivated through what I presume to be an awareness of her immense power and pre–social media humility.

"I was a bad girl from the beginning," she says. The distance between Toronto, where I live, and Vancouver, where she lives, gives way to an immediate familiarity. It is striking to me that a leader who has received numerous decorations, including a Lifetime Achievement Tribute from the Canadian Race Relations Foundation and a Congressional Gold Medal under the Clinton administration, would preface her tremendous leadership and service in this way. Maintaining a connection with my rebellious inner girl, not strictly achieving awards or notoriety, is one way I strive to grow in leadership and personal power.

For Minnijean, much of that power was seeded by her mother, Imogene Brown, a homemaker and nurse's aide who insisted she was important, a radical act of parenting in the Jim Crow era, which used laws and signs like "No Negroes or Dogs Allowed" to tell Black people otherwise. This sense of worth may have made Minnijean especially visible and targeted; her perceived uppityness and defiance were matched by her starlet beauty. She, however, shifts the attention away from herself when speaking about the Little Rock Nine: "We all went through so much; we left school assemblies with bruises, were scalded with hot water in gym locker showers, and the adults . . . I still remember the vitriol spewing from white students and adults." The National Guard was initially called in to prevent the Black students from entering the school, due to local claims of danger and disruption of peace. That was later overturned by President Eisenhower, who issued Executive Order 10730 to support the Black students' integration of the high school.

Even as a youth under siege on the sidewalk in front of her school, Minnijean understood the importance of what they were doing. "The idea of white racial superiority was refuted by their hate . . . the hate I experienced on the street leading to my high school . . . the yelling and screaming, especially the rage and crudeness of the kind of white women active in the United Daughters of the Confederacy, who raised money to erect Confederate monuments intended to remind Black people of their place in public."

While they yelled, Minnijean sweetly smiled and sometimes skipped. "Everyday I was told that I was ugly and didn't belong but deep down I knew that I was beautiful and brilliant and deserving of an education," she says. "They couldn't conceive of a Black person like me but I refused to bow my head; my expression of joy was a way of communicating defiance and my worth."

I revisit my breath to remain present during the retelling of her painful past, entire childhoods cut short by the state's inability to equitably redistribute and share space. When I inquire about her walk to school, among my most precious childhood public space rituals, even my breath fails me. Because harm was so imminent, these students were denied the walk to school. This was especially disappointing for fifteen-year-old Minnijean. "One of the reasons I wanted to attend Central High was because it was close to my home, and I could walk to school." Instead, she carpooled with other members of the Little Rock Nine or was driven in her uncle's car to conceal her identity.

Thinking back to my fifteen-year-old self, I'm not sure I would have survived the demarcated social spaces and overall uncertainty of high school without those walks of reprieve—me, Leigh, and Nicole strutting in matching pink T-shirts and headbands on the first day of high school; Donavon, who was not yet "out," spontaneously leaping through the air like Leroy from *Fame*; and exchanging confidences with my then-best-friend Stephanie. We learned at least as much on those walks to school as we did in the classroom.

Being denied the simple pleasure and right to walk to school in the U.S. and being unable to freely patronize movie theatres and restaurants under Jim Crow shaped Brown-Trickey's initial perception of Canada when she and Roy moved here: "When I first arrived in Canada in the 1980s, I thought it was almost heaven. I was concerned about the ways Pakistani women were harassed on the bus and Italian women were harassed on the streets," she says. At that time, given all that Minnijean experienced in the U.S., she didn't perceive Black people to be central to public expressions of racism.

In addition to feeling a sense of belonging in public spaces, Minnijean secured a job within a week of arriving in Canada. "I worked in a public health laboratory with overqualified immigrants who'd been physicians in their home countries," she recalls, "and I also made friends with Indigenous people and neighbours from around the world." Despite being white and a man, her husband, Roy, did not fare as well, and the couple soon moved their six children to a rural Ontario community primarily comprised of francophones and rural anglophones.

"I think I intentionally blinded myself to the anti-Black racism here," she says. There were only three or so other Black people where they lived, but she wanted to believe the best in everyone. Again, at the time, Isaiah and his siblings didn't tell their parents about the extent of racism they were dealing with in public spaces, just as the Little Rock Nine didn't tell their parents. Minnijean explains this behaviour by highlighting that, "silence is common in the psychology of racial bullying and bullying of all kinds; you're made to believe that there's something wrong with you." As the mother of a now internationally celebrated, Juno Award–winning electronic DJ-producer daughter who suffered terrible bullying at school, I feel her words land with a heavy resonance, as I imagine most parents who've supported a child through bullying would.

As the family started settling in, the veneer of Canada as *almost heaven* was tarnished. The Trickeys were heavily surveilled by neighbours and even reported to the authorities and dragged into a court battle for choosing to home-school their children. "There is no truth when it comes to Canadian history in terms of being clear about who has always been here, violations against people of colour, and anti-Blackness specifically," Minnijean says. She describes this lack of truth-telling as a "profound intentional ignorance" and draws connections between Canadian and American policies, such as the Dawes Act of 1887 in America, which authorized the federal government to further displace Native populations by partitioning their tribal lands, and Canada's Indian Act of 1876, which also systematically displaced Indigenous populations from their tribal lands. She goes on to highlight other policies that have adversely impacted racialized groups in Canada, contributing to not only economic and social stratification but underexplored place-based divides.

Although she was educated as a journalist and social worker, her lived experiences have afforded her an acute knowledge of place, spanning policy and personal experiences, the kind of knowledge needed to move us away from national moral superiority or convenient finger pointing toward Southern states to deepening our understanding of how Black bodies are distinctly yet devastatingly restricted across time, place, and cultural contexts.

I end the conversation holding sacred parts of an intertwined story between mother and son, unspoken words strewn across a geography of trauma, mutual respect, and intergenerational resilience.

–

INSTITUTED IN BRITAIN centuries ago, the vagrancy law was originally used to maintain social order by keeping everyone in their *proper place*. Today, it continues to reinforce contemporary street hierarchies through police profiling, stop and search, public transit policing, and random vendor permit checks.

Interestingly, this single law covers a wide array of "offences," such as sleeping, drinking, begging, wandering, and performing in public. And as scholar and author of *Vagrant Nation* Risa Goluboff aptly notes, the "breadth and ambiguity" of this "forgotten law" has over-empowered states and cities that have "deployed and retooled vagrancy laws for use against almost any—real or perceived, old or new—threat to public order and safety."

Anti-vagrancy laws are particularly perilous when wielded against Black people because, as numerous research studies find, Black skin, especially medium- to dark-toned Black skin, is coded as criminal. So, Black people don't need to be engaged in threatening activity in public to elicit unwanted attention from law enforcement. Because slavery shackled Black people to an exploitative economy and the plantation itself, being Black in public has always been a legally defensible cause for suspicion and state-sanctioned murder.

Law enforcement's discretionary power to approach Black people on suspicion is a continuation of historical harm and reveals a lack of understanding of the fault lines and cultural maps overlaid across urban geographies. The absence of social, spatial, and historical context has normalized the use of anti-vagrancy laws to perpetuate and condone police profiling, which disproportionately impacts Black people residing in North American cities such as Ottawa, Los Angeles, Toronto, and New York City.

Racially motivated police profiling predicated on both anti-vagrancy laws and the long-standing public space social contract is often justified as an extension of offender profiling practices that have enabled law enforcement to predict an identified offender's future sex, arson, or terrorism crimes. It is further obfuscated by proactive policing rhetoric, which is to say policing that prevents, rather than responds to, crime—a practice that, uncoincidentally, emerged in the 1960s amid the civil rights movement. This entangled enforcement discourse is intentionally designed to evoke a collective fear that contributes to a false paradigm privileging personal safety over collective human rights. This same tactic has been used post-9/11 against Muslim communities and, to a lesser extent, against street-involved populations like unhoused people, who are often characterized as a threat to local households and businesses.

Calls to both reform policing and reallocate police funding couldn't be more urgent, but there's another aspect of public space policing that rarely receives scrutiny—and it's something I refer to as citizen profiling. I suspect we avoid this issue because it implicates all of us, calling our entire public space culture into question. Whenever I hear profiling arguments solely focused on the tyranny of the police, I pose an inconvenient question: *"Who the hell is calling the police?"*

Don't get me wrong, there are situations that require intervention from properly trained and just law enforcement professionals. Having grown up in an inner-city community with persistent safety issues, I don't have the privilege of discounting the enforcement of the law, but it is exceedingly evident that a new system inclusive of critical race analysis, community care, and restorative justice must be established for Black people and other criminalized groups to be safe in public. And this new system must address citizen profiling—a term I use to describe surveillance and assertion of spatial control among everyday people—because many of the same individuals denouncing police profiling subconsciously engage in citizen profiling.

Over the past twenty years, I've witnessed the ways residents survey, judge, and call the police, bylaw officers, transit security, and condo security on people they deem suspicious. I've led hundreds of public consultation meetings related to affordable housing development, street safety design, and new parks and watched residents go from being seemingly rational humans sipping coffee and warmly greeting their neighbours to raging gatekeepers demanding that "those people," meaning anyone who isn't affluent and respectable-presenting, be barred from the public realm. I've also heard endless stories about business improvement and neighbourhood watch group members calling the police on people for perceived crimes such as dancing in public, being poor in public, and having a mental health crisis in public. What these meetings have taught me is to always listen to the streets over progressive platitudes and municipal diversity slogans.

While I love my job and have an unyielding faith that we can indeed unlearn place-based biases through education and compassion, I've come to terms with the ugly fact that many of us are quick to criminalize public space behaviours that warrant community and systemic social supports. Rather than stewarding public spaces by respecting the land and each other, we've asserted unhealthy ownership over spaces like parks and public transit, and we are constantly reading each other's bodies.

My concept of reading bodies in public spaces emerges from an exploration of human territoriality, which is related to animal territoriality—think of the fierce male South China tiger scent-marking his territory. In both animal and human contexts, territoriality is tethered to our natural sense of survival, defensiveness, and desire to personalize spaces. Among humans, territoriality is expressed through interpersonal interactions and the assertion of institutional power through administrative and spatial influence. As we navigate public spaces, we are constantly reading each other's bodies—the stagger of a group of young fans pouring into the streets after their hometown team's victory or the hyper-erect shoulders of a woman walking down a poorly lit street at night. We all search each other for nonverbal cues that inform our interactions in public spaces.

Reflect for a moment on whether you've opted to stand on the subway when there was a perfectly good seat available next to a passenger, or thought that an individual was in the "wrong" public restroom. These and countless other split-second judgments and actions are made purely by reading the facial expressions, body movements, body type, and body ornamentation—meaning tattoos, hairstyles, and clothing—of individuals in public spaces. While reading bodies is natural and can help us to assert healthy spatial boundaries that keep us safe from harm, our readings of each other are stained with stereotypes, incomplete stories about people who are different from us, and the fatal human flaw of categorization.

Our modern reading of bodies and resulting citizen profiling ironically stem, in large part, from advocates of vibrant public spaces like renowned urbanist Jane Jacobs. Jacobs's landmark book, *The Death and Life of Great American Cities*, is an inarguably brilliant work when it comes to the advocacy of diverse and walkable communities connected by a vibrant street culture. However, given that this work was written amid the civil rights, disability rights, and women's rights movements, there could have been deeper analysis about the various and often invisible barriers different types of people face. She wrote about the ballet of a "good city sidewalk" as the discordant songs of protest and grief rose from the very sites she somewhat romantically described.

Understanding that it takes many narrators to tell a complete story, I'm uninclined to be overly critical about the place-based topics she didn't write about. My contention regarding her work primarily centres on her assertion that public peace is not maintained by police but is "enforced by the people themselves." She introduces what I believe to be unintentionally dangerous public space nomenclature, such as "eyes on the street" and "natural proprietors of the street." Taking these concepts into account, we must ask ourselves:

- What are the criteria for natural proprietors of the street?
- Who gets to decide if a group or individual is a natural proprietor of the street?
- What does it tangibly mean for people to partake in enforcement and keep their eyes on the street?

–

Numerous neighbourhood watch groups across North America have been inspired by Jacobs's ideas. They have organized to educate themselves about maintaining safety and well-being in their local communities. Gathering with neighbours to explore local safety issues is not a bad thing. The problem is that if there are "natural proprietors of the street," then there must be "unnatural proprietors" that we must keep our eyes on to enforce the peace. This line of thinking contributes to conditions for resident profiling, and worse.

I would never suggest that Jacobs intentionally articulated an idea that could contribute to citizen profiling and resulting tragedies; by all accounts, she was a champion of people and cities. I wouldn't even suggest that we should discount her substantial body of work. I'm willing to concede that she, like all of us, was influenced by the corner of the street she occupied. However, because her work has profoundly shaped the way we think about public spaces, and cities more broadly, it would behoove us to advance our understanding of the power imbalances and invisibly demarcated lines that plague public spaces, and how our very identities and stories actually produce public spaces.

My inquiry into this subject led me all the way back to French Marxist philosopher Henri Lefebvre. Born in 1901, Lefebvre pioneered a critique of everyday life and the production of social space. He asserted that space was more than a material setting or cityscape, but an ever-changing, dynamic entity "produced and reproduced through human intentions" shaped by political, economic, demographic, global, and environmental forces. He also believed in the alchemy of space, meaning a recognition of the indefinite multitude of spaces, including imaginative space, layered on top of each other. Simply put, our identities and interpersonal exchanges shape the quality of public spaces in real time. I am buoyed by the possibility that despite the history of the auction block, we, Black people like myself and all people, can steward new futures. This is the good ground I lay on my personal and professional journey toward Black public joy.

PART THREE

PROTEST

As word of Michael Brown's murder was catching fire across American cities, Sarah, a travelling nurse stationed in Ferguson, Missouri, called her twin sister, April, in Lexington, Kentucky, to tell her about the young man whose body was left unceremoniously in the streets after being killed by law enforcement. April, a single mother of three—including a six-month-old whose Southern Baptist preacher father disappeared after learning about the pregnancy—began making childcare arrangements. Her parents agreed to supervise all three children. The hours that followed were a flurry of packing, organizing a carpool to Ferguson, and pumping and freezing breast milk for her baby girl. The decision to leave wasn't an easy one, but it felt like it had been made for her. She would lend her voice and, if necessary, her postpartum body to what would become one of the most heated protests in contemporary history. By the time she'd kissed her little ones goodbye and loaded up her trunk, the situation had escalated from a shooting to an uprising.

Community and court outline divergent plot lines of the tragedy. According to Officer Darren Wilson, Michael Brown was walking home with his friend, Dorian Johnson, shortly after a police dispatcher reported a "stealing in progress," referring to Brown swiping cigarillos. This claim was later refuted by a withheld video suggesting Brown was collecting the cigarillos in exchange for a small bag of weed he'd previously left with the store clerk. However, Brown's identity and these contested details were unknown to both the dispatcher and Wilson, who initiated the fatal confrontation.

Wilson reported being back in service after responding to a call involving a baby with breathing complications. Moments later, the officer, whose own mother had been repeatedly convicted of theft and cons, came across Brown and Johnson. Wilson claims the two young men were uncompliant when asked to move from the middle of the roadway onto the sidewalk and that, without provocation, Brown assaulted him through his driver side window and tried to take his gun.

Johnson's story is less tidy. He claims Wilson aggressively instructed them to move out of the roadway onto the sidewalk, and when they didn't immediately comply, the officer attempted to open his car door, which ricocheted off the bodies of the two young men. He then reached out of the window of his police car and angrily grabbed Brown around the neck. Michael Brown is not here to tell us how he ended up with a bullet through his hand, a shot in the back, and several shots to the front of his body. What we do know is that, as in so many encounters between Black men and law enforcement, Michael Brown, an unarmed recent high school graduate, ended up another lifeless Black body, his blood snaking between the sidewalk's cracks.

Following the tragedy, a United States Department of Justice report found the Ferguson Police Department guilty of engaging in a pattern of unconstitutional stops and arrests, using excessive force, creating unnecessary barriers to challenging and resolving municipal code violations, and instituting unduly harsh penalties for missed payments and court appearances. The report also determined that the police department's law enforcement actions were driven in part by "racial bias" and imposed a "disparate impact on African Americans." These and numerous other cited discriminatory practices were found to violate the First and Fourth Amendments, which, respectively, grant the right to peacefully protest and to protection against unlawful searches.

Again, the where of an injustice is as important as the injustice itself, and in this instance, the trail of state corruption and discrimination leads us to Kinloch, Missouri's first-ever Black incorporated town. Abutted by Ferguson and Berkeley—two hostile sundown towns—the small community thrived, establishing its own Black police force, Black school, and Black movie theatre. Former resident Reverend Dr. Earbie Bledsoe recalled Kinloch being a "complete city" where Black residents felt considerable pride of place.

Then, a few decades ago, the city of St. Louis started buying up land, sometimes coercing Black residents to sell, to build a new runway for its international airport. Steven Peebles, who previously lived in Kinloch, says residents were "effectively and essentially gobbled up" by the government's ambition.

The runway was never constructed, but the land grab contributed to a seismic demographic shift between the two adjacent yet profoundly divided cities. Within a couple of decades, Ferguson went from a white majority city to a Black majority city and Kinloch, once home to ten thousand residents, dwindled to a mere three hundred individuals and families who lived among shuttered public buildings and overgrown plots used as illegal dumping grounds for trash and, sometimes, dead bodies.

In the film *Where the Pavement Ends*, documentarian Jane Gillooly, a white woman who grew up in Ferguson, figuratively resurrects a roadblock that once separated Kinloch and Ferguson as a way of restaging the scene of the Michael Brown tragedy. As a child, Gillooly was unaware that, as she puts it, "Ferguson was a closed community," until she ventured out to Suburban Avenue. There, she first saw the roadblock. "A metal corrugated guardrail cemented into the ground like something you see running along the side of the highway or at the end of a dead-end road." Such roadblocks were intentionally used to entrench racial divides and resentment across the United States. A Black elder featured in the documentary recalls, "The one thing I remember was that we were angry . . . A lot of people don't get it." Public infrastructure, like the guardrails referenced in Gillooly's documentary, as well as highways, bridges, and railways, cemented social hierarchies between Black and white people in public spaces across North America.

And although largely unacknowledged, these and other types of public infrastructure can instill anger in Black communities, constituting a pervasive form of urban trauma—a term coined by Dr. Maysa Akbar. While an inanimate piece of infrastructure cannot be held accountable for Michael Brown's death, examining the histories and stories associated with public spaces helps us to understand how the conditions for conflict were written into the asphalt long before Michael Brown was felled on a city street.

–

UPON ARRIVING IN Ferguson, April and her friends were greeted by the charred remains of the QuikTrip gas station, which she describes as "a memorial site outside of the war zone." Flowers and written messages stretched the length of the street. Mourners held each other up when their knees threatened to buckle under the weight of the injustice. Others wept alone. The anger would come later.

April recalls marching from Canfield Drive, the street where Brown was killed, to the Ferguson police station alongside Michael Brown's mother, who, according to April, was wearing high heels while carrying his toddler sister most of the route. April was awed by this woman's strength—by the strength of Black mothers forced to march down to the school, the mall, and the recreation centre to advocate for their children. The intensity of the moment increased with each step toward the police station.

The protestors found themselves face to face, breath to breath, with menacing members of the National Guard, who, based on reports obtained by CNN, referred to protestors as "enemy forces" and "adversaries" on domestic soil. Joshua Williams, an eighteen-year-old protestor, confronted them, tears streaming down his face, asking, "Am I going to be next?"

April says his question was met with contemptuous silence from the police, provoking a swell of anger that threatened to breach the small gap between the protestors and the National Guard, between peaceful protest and explosive confrontation. The screaming and wailing were incoherent—resistance became its own language, strictly understood by the protestors.

It was in this moment, marked by risk and rapture, that April found her calling as a civil rights organizer and protestor.

She would make three more trips between Lexington and Ferguson to march for Michael Brown and her own babies, and later she answered a national call issued by the Movement for Black Lives and received training in peaceful protest tactics and community organizing.

Following her time in Ferguson, she began working in her home city with an organization called Stop Mass Incarceration Network Kentucky that contributed to compelling Lexington law enforcement to wear body cameras. She worked with Lexington community markets to organize produce pop-ups that provided low-income residents with organic fruits and vegetables on a sliding scale. She travelled to Cleveland to protest the killing of twelve-year-old Tamir Rice, who was murdered for being a kid with a toy gun.

In 2015, April received the Peacemaker of the Year award from the Central Kentucky Council for Peace and Justice and was granted a coveted spot in the Highlander Research and Education Center. She contributed to and achieved all of this without stable employment or a partner to help with her three children. Even with these impressive community contributions and accolades, she was not entirely embraced by those on the front lines or making change within institutions.

–

BY THE TIME I travelled to Lexington, Kentucky, to lead a placemaking project focused on the redevelopment of Cheapside Market, a Confederate monument site, April had a reputation for being an angry activist and protestor, frequently taking to the streets amplifying social justice issues.

I was introduced to her during a tour of a vibrant co-working space with a brewery and community urban greenhouse on the ground floor. I don't recall our brief exchange or the colour of her blouse. What I do remember is the feeling of her eyes following me down the stairs and my trepidation about the complex and highly sensitive process ahead.

There were disconcerting unknowns inherent in this project, including the very real threat of violence. The Confederate monuments had been removed under the cloak of night and stored in an undisclosed location. Local activists confided that they'd received threats from white supremacists, including the actual Ku Klux Klan. I took these threats seriously, given that a recent protest revolving around Confederate monuments in Charlottesville had resulted in the killing of a young white woman named Heather Heyer.

Described as the epicentre of the slave trade in Kentucky, Cheapside was where countless individuals—granted first names only—were brought to the auction block to settle their owners' debts, bequeathed to their owners' family members, and bundled and sold with their owners' bedsheets and chickens. Learning that they were not only sold, but sold alongside animals and objects, broke something inside me. Notwithstanding the sacredness of all beings, I couldn't comprehend Black life being diminished to that of a chicken or, worse, an inanimate object.

As a Black person living in a Canadian city, my intergenerational trauma isn't ignited on my way to the grocery store or park. I have been shielded from places like a major auction site or former plantation ground. I encountered both for the first time in Lexington. This isn't to suggest that slavery was not a reality here in Canada. And unlike many Canadians, I'm uninclined to detract from our own hostile cultural and geographic landscapes by pointing to Americans. We've all inherited unfathomable histories. It's just that nothing could have prepared me for the embodied remembering that happened while I stood at a site where my ancestors—some of whom could have had the same tribal, linguistic, and place-based origins as myself—were publicly fated to unspeakable violence and what Langston Hughes described as "a dream deferred."

These ancestral aches were countered by the beauty of the community. Two white activists, whose windows had been busted out by locals opposed to their Black Lives Matter lawn sign, invited me over for dinner. Their home had served as a refuge for an inner circle of Black activists who sometimes needed respite from the demands and discouragements of sustaining their advocacy efforts to have the monuments removed. We decided to extend the dinner invitation to a couple of these activists and other residents I was getting acquainted with.

I welcomed the opportunity to gather in an intimate space, which is my approach when initiating high-stakes placemaking projects. I find that dinner tables, sidewalk storytelling sessions, and spread-out blankets in public parks create the conditions for slower, more generative conversations. Piling hundreds of people in a hot room, with sweaty plastic chairs and foldout tables stacked with swampy coffee and two-for-one pizza with a sad single layer of cheese, has never created the conditions for productive public space conversations. Sitting in spaces small enough to properly interpret inflection and sense the intent behind imperfectly stated perspectives establishes ground for grace.

When I approached the front door of the home, I was a bit unnerved by the remnants of the broken window, but I slowly eased into the promise of the evening as the husband, a gentle and genuine musician-farmer, played actual vinyl on the family record player as I co-prepared my grandmother's curry dish, chatting with his talented writer wife. Their young son, with an odd and virtuous name, excitedly ran back and forth, uprooting herbs from their garden. A couple of hours later, the screen door announced the arrival of our guests, who were greeted by an aromatic cloud drifting from the kitchen into the front room. April and her twin sister, Sarah, were among them.

Everyone greeted me warmly, but there was an uneasiness between the twins and the two Black male activists largely credited for the removal of the monuments. By the time eight or so of us sat down to eat the spicy baked chicken and hefty heaping of vegan curry atop fragrant Caribbean rice and peas—my grandmother would be so proud that I found a way to integrate our culture into my professional practice—the tension was undeniable. And so, while pouring a glass of wine, I asked what was wrong, in the direct manner with which people with Jamaican grandmothers lean into discomfort.

This question, as with all genuine inquiry, cut through to the conversation's core. April and Sarah immediately seized the opportunity to share their concerns with the two Black male activists about what they perceived to be an exclusion of Black single mothers like themselves from the organizing efforts.

This critique is common. Civil rights movements have often centred heterosexual Black men, oftentimes erasing Black women, Black 2SLGBTQ+ individuals, and Black disabled people.

Situations like the one at hand, too delicate to detail, are often critiqued as Black people's inability to cooperate in the interest of our collective liberation. But power imbalances such as patriarchy and ableism exist across all communities. Protestors tend to be activists seeking justice and are judged more harshly for failing to meet increasingly unforgiving progressive standards.

To further complicate matters, institutions such as the media and municipalities tend to latch on to what I refer to as the individual protagonist protestor—think Mahatma Gandhi or Gloria Steinem—to build both narratives and negotiations around. While protagonist protestors make many valid contributions, their voices and efforts often overshadow those of a much broader group of people working to advance actions and movements. The erasure of this silenced and sometimes sacrificial collective inevitably leads to internal conflict. Understanding these delicate dynamics within groups and the external forces that exacerbate them, I sat silently, holding space for the discomfort hovering above the wooden dining room table. As folks sipped their last bit of red wine and ate their final bites of food, I felt an appreciation for all of them. But perhaps because of the way I could sense a soft heart beneath what some may perceive as a tough exterior, I felt a special connection to April.

My days in Kentucky were filled with neighbourhood tours and conversations in corner nooks of locally owned coffee shops. I met with esteemed senior municipal leaders like Glenn Brown, who recalled walking beneath the monuments as a boy, and Sean Gladding, a punk rock pastor who loved a good brew and the hope of the gospels. And I was heartened by local initiatives like Unlearn Fear + Hate, a creative place-based project led by scholar-activists Kremena Todorova and Kurt Gohde alongside their frequent collaborator Hoda Shalash.

But the most powerful moment of my orientation occurred at Cheapside, with April. Beneath a thin blanket of nightfall, she asked, "Can you feel the spirit of our ancestors here?" There was something about the gentleness of her tone and how she embraced me in the question. I'd never been asked to lay down my intellectual perceptions and place-based processes in quite that manner before. I bowed my head and my shoulders and allowed myself to embody, I mean really feel, the site, and there they were. "Yes," I said. "Yes, I can feel our ancestors." This is the moment I truly met the April beneath the shield of her anger.

–

BRITTNEY COOPER, AUTHOR of *Eloquent Rage*, explains how the expression of rage—this often pathologized and suppressed emotion—has infused American political movements with undeniable potency. My own anger has propelled me beyond increasingly impermeable social margins, whether professionally or in elite public spaces, which at times attempt to attack the validity of my very presence, ideas, and irrepressible self-worth. Boundary-defying anger has also prompted me to speak up and act on behalf of others experiencing forms of place-based injustices, such as homelessness and gender-based street harassment.

At the same time, as I've grown older, I've recognized the ways that public expressions of anger have left me exhausted and disconnected from my purpose. I often reflect on Toni Morrison's brilliant revelation about the "very serious function of racism" being a "distraction," which compels you to explain "your reason for being." Similarly, I view the constant cycle of public expressions of Black anger, most pronounced in protests, as a distraction from Black people's public joy.

The same anger required to withstand the physical and psychological impacts of sustained public protest can create calcification around the heart and conflict within Black communities. Reductive perceptions of Black people as angry and resilient become reinforced, further contributing to racial discrimination. To experience joy, public or otherwise, all humans must be provided with the space to express tenderness, vulnerability, grief, anxiety, uncertainty, and other emotions that make us wholly and holy human. Yet for Black people, carving out joyful and dignified space has, from the very beginning of our enslavement, been almost exclusively achieved through protest.

The first formal rebellion initiated by enslaved African Americans occurred in 1663 in Gloucester, Virginia; closer to home, in 1734, an indomitable African Canadian woman, Marie-Joseph Angélique, set fire to the home of the man who enslaved her, burning down much of Old Montreal. Historians estimate that 250 revolts occurred in America before slavery was abolished, which doesn't include rebellions across the diaspora, like Haitians gaining their independence in the early 1800s and Maroons in Jamaica, the island of my birth, establishing liberated communities in the interior mountains of the island.

These and many other forms of public protest have, throughout history and the Black diaspora, been culturally defined by a distinct dichotomy of joy and righteous rage.

Take, for instance, Mardi Gras in New Orleans. Today the festival is known for embracing the city's Indigenous, African American, and European cultural heritage, but in the late 1800s it was used as a political platform for reinforcing white supremacy through its floats, public performances, and displays.

In the early 1900s, Black groups like the Zulu Social Aid and Pleasure Club infiltrated the festival wearing grass skirts and painted faces as a way of subverting racist stereotypes while embracing Afrocentric aesthetics. Although contested, this was particularly noteworthy for some because colourism—a form of internalized racism falsely ascribing beauty and intellectual capacity only to lighter-skinned Black people—prevented many people in our community from accessing fraternities and social spaces if they couldn't pass the paper bag test (measuring Black skin in relation to a brown paper bag) or the comb test (measuring the kinkiness of Black hair in relation to hair associated with whiteness). This disruption to the Mardi Gras parade and embrace of Black aesthetics were truly revolutionary. They occurred decades before the civil rights and "Black is beautiful" movements. It was also incredibly bold given that New Orleans didn't pass legislation to desegregate Mardi Gras until 1992.

Another example of joyful public protest is Caribana, which takes place in Toronto. The parade is the largest Caribbean carnival in North America, introduced to Canadians in 1967 as part of the country's centennial celebration. This multi-day street festival features mas bands adorned in lavish cultural costumes—expertly constructed from vibrant materials, feathers, and glitter topped with regal headpieces—along with steel pan players making melodies on an instrument that was once outlawed. Together with over a million attendees, these and other cultural artists and animators awaken the streets' vibrancy. The roots of this electrifying and, for some, sensual celebration are found in resistance. In the late eighteenth century, enslaved individuals abducted to the islands of Trinidad and Tobago ignited a fiery riot, protesting slavery. They sang and played instruments, connecting with their ancestors while charting a course toward freedom.

In addition to these histories of joyful rebellion, my admiration for protestors was cultivated by reading about the 1976 Soweto uprising, back when the now universally beloved Nelson Mandela was regarded as a terrorist. Twenty thousand young students marched to maintain their Indigenous languages in their schools, and hundreds of them were slaughtered by a vicious military force. Around the same time I learned about this atrocity, I witnessed the brutality of the 1990 Oka Crisis, led by unrelenting Mohawk land defenders who erected a barricade to block the expansion of a golf course. Many years later, I would have the opportunity to speak with Waneek Horn-Miller, the teenager turned Olympian who was stabbed in the chest by a soldier's bayonet. The doctor who eventually treated her—she was held in custody for twenty-two whole hours with a hole next to her heart—told her that if the bayonet had entered a centimetre to either side, she would have died.

I was deeply moved by the courage and sacrifices of these young protestors. My interest expanded: the Stonewall Uprising to protect the right of 2SLGBTQ+ people to freely gather and express themselves, the Tiananmen Square protests initiated by Chinese students who spoke out for economic reforms and freedoms, and the Chipko movement in India led by the original tree-hugging women who fought for their right to protect trees and other natural resources.

As I grew older, I became increasingly aware of the relationship between place, protest, and the tangible expression of a living democracy. For the freedoms and rights inherent in democratic state systems to be more than an ideology or virtue, places like parks, streets, and markets are required for practice. And while I have a healthy respect for the power of protest, it should not be the primary practice or tangible evidence of a living democracy. In fact, a continual cycle of public protest rather than public joy is an indictment of our democratic systems.

Public spaces should indeed foster democratic practices such as generative debate and the expression of dissatisfaction to create social change. It is also true that these sites should honour our individuality while transcending the constructed bounds of those very same identity boxes—race, gender, and class—to foster mutual respect and care. Public spaces should be places that nurture curiosity about our built and natural environments, and provide us with a daily sense of delight. These too are the public practices of democracy, not strictly protest.

In addition to analyzing the public practices of democracy, I began to develop a critique of protest—not the type of conservative critique focused on superficial civility or respectability politics amid injustice. I was genuinely curious about the frequency of sustainable structural changes resulting from public protests, and the adverse impacts on protestors who often sacrifice safety, family, and economic stability. Ironically, the privilege of critiquing public protest—reflecting on its history, power, and complicated joy—is a result of courageous protestors, past and present. I came across Peter Marcuse, a Berlin-born lawyer and urban planning scholar who participated in the Freedom Summer project—an initiative focused on registering African American voters residing in Mississippi. He cautioned against fetishizing space, noting, "The concern with the occupied space is a means to an end, and only one means among others, not the end itself." He explained that occupied spaces are not the prize but rather "the terrain on which the battle takes place." While I disagree with his assessment that space is not the prize—for people relegated to the margins, space is always a part of the prize—I do agree that protest is "not the end itself." I firmly believe that public protest is part of a constellation of actions and aspirations, which are difficult to address when protestors are so frequently forced onto the streets.

Since the abolition of slavery, protest has been the primary communicative mode between Black communities and the state, just as it was during the era of slavery itself. Black protestors are often either valorized or vilified. Neither of these two poles, focused on individuals, creates the conditions for structural interrogation. How can the same state violating Black people's rights in public spaces also issue permits, dispatch police, and establish curfews for peaceful protests? This is indicative of a continued lack of spatial and democratic rights. Sure, democracy now grants Black people the right to protest, but doesn't democracy also have a responsibility to address the issues igniting ongoing protests? The facilitation of Black protest feeds media outlets and political agendas across partisan lines while leaving entire Black communities starved for justice.

We must ask ourselves, "Why, since emancipation, has the state sanctioned Black protests rather than addressing systemic issues prohibiting Black people's rights and public joy?"

Such fundamental questions form the premise of my critique of the constant cycle of Black protest.

Black people have marched enough, been fire-hosed by police officers enough, bitten by attack dogs enough, and ironically spat on by those demanding our civility enough. Many Black scholars and activists have argued that the public expression of Black anger is an act of courage, a wellness practice, a form of creative expression, and even a spiritual virtue. I completely concur. Our righteous rage is a form of cultural alchemy and confirmation that the enslaver's whip did not strip us of our sense of self-worth. The debt owed to those on the front lines is beyond monetary currency. Yet, I cannot shake my critique and concern. The constant cycle of public protest casts Black bodies like placards with faded messages and torn corners, piled as leaves fallen from trees, left naked and vulnerable, awaiting winter.

At the same time, protestors count every moment of joy, whether large or small, a battle won.

April recalls the time she was in Cleveland for a Movement for Black Lives gathering, which was attended by protestors from multiple cities along with mothers whose children had been killed in public spaces. As at most protests, numerous police officers were in attendance. A group of them apprehended a young boy, who looked no older than fourteen, on suspicion that he was drinking alcohol from a cup. The police put the child in the back seat of a cruiser to transport him elsewhere rather than trying to locate his mother, who was also at the protest. In response, the crowd created a human barricade, fortified by the conviction that another baby would not be lost on their watch. April and the other protestors obstructed the vehicle long enough for the young boy's mother to retrieve him from the police. At that moment, the crowd broke out into the Kendrick Lamar song "Alright." It doesn't always end this way—hell, I imagine that it doesn't often end this way. But April is adamant that when it does, it's a form of "public joy."

In addition to protestors being heard and experiencing instances of collective impact, April has highlighted to me how stewarded protest sites are spaces of healing and mutual care. When sites are occupied by seasoned, well-trained protestors like April, considerable thought goes into spatial planning and maintenance. This often begins with engaging Indigenous Peoples familiar with the history of the site. Also, vulnerable groups such as sex workers and unhoused people are considered to ensure that occupied protest sites do not inadvertently displace or harm them. Stations or zones such as a welcome table with educational materials, healthy food sharing stations, and commemorative street altars are established. Protestors often create cleaning and unarmed security schedules. In some cases, they pray over or sage occupied sites.

As a placemaker, I'm impressed by the ways protestors reimagine public spaces, intuitively drawing on design principles such as gentle barrier control, maintenance, and temporary mixed use. Their thoughtful approach is often overlooked by media intent on reporting on looting and property destruction, resulting in hyper-criticism of protestors rather than of the structural issues they are protesting to resolve. This ingenuity, modelled at many occupied sites, is emblematic of the humanity of protestors and their regard for all people and places.

–

SEVERAL YEARS AGO, April was pulled over by a police officer while driving. When he asked her to produce insurance, she panicked and posed as her twin sister, Sarah—a choice that still causes tension between the pair—to avoid paying a fine she couldn't afford or worse. She was found out and immediately remanded into custody.

Upon her arrival at the detention facility, she was placed on suicide watch and thrown in solitary confinement. April contends she was, naturally, distressed but not suicidal. However, what she describes as the "fucking torture" of weeks in solitary confinement significantly impacted her mental well-being. At first, she counted the days beneath an unyielding bright light, yearning for green space or something to read. In the mornings, her mattress was taken away from her, so she sat on the floor with nothing but her thoughts. She worried about her three children, even though they were being lovingly cared for by her parents, and wondered where the revolutionaries were to rescue her. Soon the days blurred together, so she stopped trying to keep count and gave up waiting for good news.

Instead, she focused on the probability that she would do the kind of time Black protestors receive for making a mistake while being known troublemakers. She thought of her young acquaintance Joshua Williams, who'd confronted the National Guard in Ferguson. After protesting for Michael Brown, he stayed in the streets to help amplify concerns about the fatal shooting of Antonio Martin, another young Black male. Unlike with Brown, the evidence confirms that Martin had a weapon, but protestors, still raw from the previous local tragedy, demanded to know why the officer in question approached the Black youth in the first place and conveniently forgot to wear the body camera he had been issued earlier that day.

Although Joshua was only eighteen years old, he was a beloved and well-known protestor. While fighting for answers, Joshua allegedly stole a bag of chips and lit a trash can on fire. He was sentenced to eight years in prison, despite not having a criminal record, and the community heeded the heavy-handed penalty, which was meant as a message to Black protestors. He is the only Ferguson protestor still in prison. While he was incarcerated, his mother died of cancer.

As it did for Joshua, Ferguson spurred April's activism. Sitting on the concrete and metal floor of her cell, April prepared herself for a fate like Joshua's—a protestor harshly sentenced to send a message.

One night, while sleeping on her battered mattress, April had a dream. I smile when she begins her story like this, because Black people across time and place weave dreamscapes into lived realities. Literally every Black woman I know who's over forty years old often begins serious stories and revelations with "I had a dream . . ."

"I saw my cousin who'd been dead for decades," she told me. April went on to explain that he'd passed more than twenty years ago, but she held on to a fondness for him because when she'd become pregnant in college, he made her feel like it wasn't a moral failing. This cousin reassured her that everything was going to be okay. On this particular night, he crossed unknown spatial realms to deliver a message she didn't have words for, but when she woke up, she knew someone else in her family had died.

That same day, an officer who didn't usually stop at her cell paused to have a brief conversation. She told him about her dream and pleaded for the special privilege of making a call while in solitary confinement. It was granted, and the moment she heard a voice on the other end of the phone, she said, "Dad, who's dead?" Given her situation, April's father lied and assured her the family was well, but she later learned that her uncle had indeed passed just prior to her dream.

After several days in solitary confinement, April entered the general population of the prison. Being released from confinement had its own distinct challenges. She had a shingles outbreak due to the stress, and the medication caused her to lose handfuls of her beautiful dark wavy hair. The other women inmates taunted her and stole things from her. One woman gathered April's clothes, doused them in ketchup, and left the pile in the middle of the pod, claiming it was menstrual blood. Soon rumours circulated that that inmate wanted to fight, and although April was ill and didn't want that kind of trouble, she couldn't, as she put it, "bitch out." Before the inmate could make good on her threats, she was placed in solitary confinement—a pain April knew well.

By that time, April had earned enough good behaviour merits to be assigned the duty of conducting nighttime checks. It only paid five dollars per week, but it extended her time outside her cell, which she desperately needed to recover from the trauma of solitary confinement. Knowing how unbelievably terrifying it was to be slowly disappeared behind the metal door, April often paused at her adversary's cell to chat. She learned the woman was a lesbian and that she was concerned about her ill mother at home. When I ask if they made amends before April was released, she says, "I wouldn't call it that because I knew that she might still come for me the moment she was out . . . but the thing is . . . I couldn't walk by her cell."

This is the imperfect, tender-hearted April I know.

–

IN THE SPRING of 2021, I was saddened but unsurprised to hear that prolonged protest and community organizing had taken a toll on April. She was *away* and regaining her wellness. I wept, thinking her collapse was inevitable. Knowing that April had previously spent time incarcerated, I worried about how her stay, albeit this time at a very different kind of facility, might adversely impact her. Before I could spiral down the hole of hopeless scenarios, she reappeared on my Facebook feed—among the memes and middle-aged people's conspiracy theories—demanding justice for Breonna Taylor. Breonna was a paramedic from April's state of Kentucky whose future was shattered by a police officer's bullet.

Following months of protests and an aggressive online campaign fuelled by high-profile African American leaders like activist Tamika Mallory and Oprah Winfrey, who gave up the cover of *O Magazine* for the first time since its inception, the police officers in the case were absolved from wrongdoing in Breonna Taylor's death. However, Officer Brett Hankison was charged with three counts of first-degree wanton endangerment because his bullet was found lodged in a neighbour's wall. The state deemed the wall, an inanimate object, more worthy of justice than a Black woman's body. I thought back to standing in Lexington's local archives, holding bills of sale for enslaved people sold alongside inanimate objects like chairs and blankets.

Understanding our collective outrage and grief, I still wondered why April felt personally compelled to return to the streets so soon after her personal crisis. She told me Brett Hankison, fired following the Breonna Taylor shooting, had previously been let go from the Lexington Police Department for "extreme violations," and his own supervisor had recommended against his future reemployment. Although the bullet that killed Breonna Taylor wasn't discharged from his gun, April wonders if she might be alive if he hadn't been present that day. No one can say for sure.

After co-leading multiple marches demanding justice, April decided to drive to Injustice Park in downtown Louisville, so-called by protestors for its proximity to the jail and county prosecutor's office. In response to the protests against Breonna's death, the city imposed curfews and brought out the tanks. Similar public protest repression tactics were used right across the country in cities like Oakland and Baltimore.

I admire April's commitment and resilience. At the same time, I'm concerned about her and about the overall sustainability of being in the streets, on the front lines of rage and risk, as often as she is. She tells me that protesting does take its toll and that "the community that you're advocating for often doesn't return care . . . I said I was not okay and begged people to help carry the load. This has to be said even if it makes me look weak or fragile." Asking for help and thinking about reciprocity are essential for continuing to protest.

–

APRIL IS UNWELL. Again. But this time, she is *sick* sick. After months of being both unheard and misdiagnosed, April has been in and out of the hospital since experiencing Ramsay Hunt syndrome. She has suffered an infection in the connective tissue around her neck, breathing challenges requiring the use of a ventilator, chronic shingles, and partial temporary paralysis. At one point, her physiotherapist suspected that she'd been walking around for a month with a broken elbow. April was unfazed. That was her exact word.

While she's currently unable to be in the streets, she continues to organize online. She shares insights about gaps in the American healthcare system and links to resources for others experiencing similar challenges. She amplifies local causes and continues to call community members to action in between posts featuring uplifting music by artists like Brittany Howard. I take a sliver of solace in the fact that she's asked for help, something she told me she felt shame about a few years ago. She's requested donations for medical supplies and a move into a new accessible residence. I send money, prayers, and a bit of unsolicited advice about prioritizing her wellness.

Roberta K. Timothy, a public health scholar, finds that racialized trauma can result in serious health issues such as "diabetes, high blood pressure, heart attack, cancer and low birth rates." The authors of a paper titled "Witnessing Modern America: Violence and Racial Trauma" assert that the psychological consequences of repeatedly witnessing anti-Black public violence not only impact victims, but "the trauma emanates outwards like ripples of water through the members of their communities." Regardless of how we resist, or whether we resist at all, I am terrified for April . . . for all of us.

–

THE PROJECT IN Cheapside concluded with a Witnessing Circle—a final convening I conceived to collectively honour the lives of enslaved African Americans and to further entrench an approach to place-based healing for the city. The considerations guiding the development of the process were predicated on multiple factors. First and foremost, I didn't want to lead a process wherein Black people were solely burdened with reconciling the site's history or retraumatized. I wanted to find a way for white people to tangibly participate in the process as a way of constructively redirecting, and perhaps even eliminating, feelings of guilt or defensiveness that arise when reconciling the histories of these types of public places. Thinking about the city's current demographics, I also sought to find a way to include community members who were neither Black nor white. I figured that a place-based reconciliation process that truly included everyone would help to establish the foundation for a reimagined public space that truly included everyone.

With these goals in mind, I worked with the municipality and other client partners to secure a theatre space located within the library close to the Cheapside Market. I gathered a group of community members who'd been deeply engaged in the larger placemaking project. A transgender student leader attending the University of Kentucky. A retired small business owner and environmental activist. A longtime public sector leader. A young Muslim woman active in her mosque and broader community. These and other community members were each assigned one of those bills of sale to read—the ones that those of us working on the project had found in the archives all those months ago, equating Black people to physical property.

A young white urban farmer and mid-career Black archivist had gone through the collection to select the bills. The Witnessing Circle began with an onstage conversation between the three of us. We explored the archival gathering process and the importance of working together to reconcile and heal places like the Cheapside Market. We spoke about the positive personal impacts of sharing the labour and building a relationship across different sides of an incredibly entangled and painful history. This conversation was punctuated by a soul-stirring rendition of "A Change Is Gonna Come." And as the vocalist ended with, "It's been a long time comin' . . . ", the twelve or so community members I'd gathered prepared to step into the spotlight and read the bills of sale.

April was selected to open the witnessing segment of the ceremony by honouring an enslaved woman named Elizabeth; no last name, as was customary. She wore a striking emerald-green wrap dress and a subtle pink lip gloss. Her beauty was always evident, but on this evening, she'd taken extra care to prepare for the ritual honouring our ancestors. When she stepped out of our group semicircle into the spotlight, she read every detail concerning the sale of Elizabeth as though it was a sacred text.

This is the indomitable and beautiful April I know.

PART FOUR

SACRED SPACE

In the fall of 2020, Chukwuwuikem Peter Nnamdi Vincent Opara took me back to his boyhood on the Path of the Old Ones. Chukwuwuikem (savour his name slowly: *Choo-kwoo-wee-khem*) goes by Ikem. He explains his middle name away: "Cause, you know, Catholicism and such." He grew up in the homeland of the indigenous Igbo people, located in Nigeria's southeastern region. When his father, Sylvester Ndukamma—pronounced with a lingering *n*—Opara, the third son of twelve children, migrated to the city, he sent money back to the family to clear a piece of land for the construction of a home. This was and continues to be a common practice for Black people on the continent and throughout the African diaspora, exemplifying successful urban migration. Ikem's uncle, the eldest brother, was the first to establish himself in the city and had already built a house close to the family compound. Fortunately, there was still some space left for his father to begin building his own house. However, when plans were drawn up to construct the first two-storey building on his family's compound, Ikem's dad, Sylvester, was dissuaded from proceeding in a particular location. Ikem explains, "The elders advised against building his home atop the Path of the Old Ones to avoid disrupting the route of the spirits." This path, deemed sacred by the villagers, is part of a network of roads that have been in Ikem's village for generations. The section that runs through his family's compound is approximately 150 metres long and wide enough that he and his friends could play, but too narrow for a bicycle or moped to pass without them needing to step out of the way.

Villagers use the path to access natural ponds fed by groundwater and rainwater. It connects them to a church and community meeting hall. As in most rural places, residential homes and community amenities are not organized on a grid, so villagers have multiple routes through their communities, which is an asset during wars and rainy-season floods. The path is part of an unvanquished ecological web, where the organic flow of bodies, spirits, and layers of time is respected. Sylvester Opara reconsidered his plans. Like villagers before him, Ikem's father respected the advice of the elders.

To give me a sense of what this sacred place looks like today, Ikem entrusts me with a video of his father's funeral procession. Smoke from cannons ascends from rich clay-coloured earth. There is a procession of people, including a woman wearing a top hat and bow tie, carrying a bouquet of flowers.

Six or so men, whose beautiful dark skin is complemented by white suits, carry Sylvester's body in a walnut and gold casket. An elder with a feather peeking out from his headwrap smiles widely, professing that Opara was his best friend. Despite the crisp air and leaves changing colour in the courtyard outside my loft, I can almost feel the sultry African sun against my face.

Ikem also shares a photo with me. There is a young boy leaning against a fence post at the entrance of the ancestral home his father built all those years ago. A little to the right of him, beyond a woman wearing a multicoloured hat, I catch a sliver of the Path of the Old Ones.

Ikem likes to imagine his father, reunited with other family members, strolling along the path—perhaps sharing an embrace and a good story, snacking on soursop. "My papa takes walks along the path just as he did when he was on this side of the universe," says Ikem. He believes, as I do, that spirits of those who have passed exist in another realm. I'm moved contemplating how, in upholding the sacred placemaking practices of his ancestors in life, Sylvester Opara created a way back to his Creator.

"The Path of the Old Ones endures and is cared for by young people in the village who spend many joy-filled days running from the home of one relative to the other barefoot, as I and many have done before me," Ikem says. Despite immigrating to Canada decades ago, he can summon a sense of safety and belonging reminiscing about the Path of the Old Ones. "It is that sense of being completely at home and safe that I believe emanates from sacred spaces." And then he says something that I will never forget. "This, too, is your birthright."

His words, weighted with generosity, were particularly healing for me. As someone geographically separated from the African continent for centuries, I'd never imagined having knowledge of a sacred place like the Path of the Old Ones, let alone having it extended to me as a birthright. While I have access to Black sacred spaces here, in the U.S., and in Jamaica, being invited to reclaim a sacred space on a part of the African continent where many of my ancestors were stolen from was a salve.

Within my practice, I have approached the spatial and spiritual disconnection from the continent much like a cultural artisan. When producing textiles, the yarn that runs vertically up and down a loom and that determines the strength of the fabric is called a warp. A broken warp is generally discarded. However, some weavers secure a fresh length of yarn and use a sewing pin or T-pin to secure it to the broken line. When thinking about Black people and sacred spaces and practices, the metaphor of weaving broken and brand-new threads together as a way of extending reverence to those of us directly from the continent and those of us descended from enslaved individuals resonates with me. The notion that there is equal value in the original broken threads and the brand-new threads feels both culturally and spiritually reparative. For all people, this is a way of acknowledging the past while making space for the present and future, from both personal and placemaking perspectives.

The idea of interweaving the past and the present as a form of resilience and being is historically aligned with the ways enslaved Africans carried knowledge of their sacred places and practices with them across the Atlantic Ocean through memory and mythmaking. From libation—a drink, often alcoholic, poured to recognize ancestors during public gatherings—to adorning oneself with special stones to cultivate safety and positive energy when navigating public spaces, many sacred placemaking practices from the African continent have been preserved.

My own grandmother spoke of numerous sacred public space practices without being aware of their African origins. For instance, she would speak about the practice of saving and planting the placenta and umbilical cord of a newborn baby at the foot of a tree. As a youth, I attributed what then sounded like a strange practice to Jamaican culture. Then I heard this practice referenced by Black people from other Caribbean islands and started to explore its origins.

I learned that in many African cultures, the placenta is buried at the foot of trees. In fact, in Burkina Faso, the term *zan boku* means "the place where the placenta is buried." In Buganda, a Bantu kingdom in Uganda, inhabitants wrap the baby's placenta in plantain leaves and the mother buries it at the base of a palm tree. The baby's sex determines the type of palm tree where the plantain-leaf-covered placenta is buried. If the baby is a boy, the placenta is planted at the base of a palm tree used to produce beer, and if the baby is a girl, the placenta is planted at the base of a palm tree producing edible fruit. After the placenta is planted, the tree is deemed sacred until the fruit ripens, at which time the baby and its paternal grandmother are permitted to approach. The grandmother returns to collect the harvest, which is used to create beer or a fruit dish for a sacred feast.

In the Kenyan Luo culture, the placenta of a girl is buried on the left-hand side of her mother's house, and the placenta of a boy is buried on the right-hand side of the house. This is in keeping with the Luo's cosmological and symbolic system, which associates the left side with impermanence and vulnerability and the right side with permanence and authority. The thinking here is that marriage will eventually make girls impermanent tribal members while boys are expected to grow up to stay and propagate patriarchal authority. The Kikuyu residing in Kenya, believing the placenta symbolizes attachment and fertility, plant it in an uncultivated field to bind the baby to its homelands and ancestors. Igbo people, like Ikem and his family, residing in Ghana and Nigeria regard the placenta as the deceased twin of the living baby and afford it full burial rights. While aspects of these rituals may reinforce gender binaries and roles, they are beautiful examples of sacred place-based practices.

Connecting the sacred place-based practice of planting the placenta at the foot of a tree in Jamaica to similar place-based practices across the African continent made me feel more known to myself, much like Ikem sharing the story of the Path of the Old Ones and his very birthright with me. Like all Black people's place-based connections, this feeling isn't without its complications.

When thinking of trees, a sacred site and symbol across numerous cultures and countries, I'm reminded of the powerful activist statement at the core of "Strange Fruit," a song recorded by Billie Holiday in 1939. This song is derived from a poem, penned a couple of years prior to its recording, about lynchings—a white supremacist public spectacle in which a white mob accuses and brutally punishes an individual Black person of a crime without due process. These public killings primarily involved violent and depraved public acts of torture, sexual violation, combustion, decapitation, and desecration. The wreckage of this Southern ritual was limp, unrecognizable Black bodies, like ripe fruit ready to be plucked from the vine. Lynchings were pervasive throughout the nineteenth and twentieth centuries, and the song was considered an anthem of the civil rights movement.

Carmen Mays is a Southern urbanist. "I'm not talkin' 'bout Atlanta or Georgia," she says. "I'm from Birmingham, the deep Deep South." She takes me beneath the song's lyrics: "The vestiges of slavery and public acts of racism can be felt in the heat and humidity of the air we're all breathin' down here." Carmen refuses to rush, or sharply cut off a single syllable, as she explains that towering willow trees and magnificent magnolias offer shade and respite while symbolizing Black struggle. In Birmingham, once described by Dr. Martin Luther King Jr. as the most segregated city in America, this dichotomy doesn't stop at the farthest sprawling tree root.

This tension is pervasive throughout the U.S., where the trauma of lynchings remains lodged as collective memory in many Black bodies. While I was leading one of many community engagement sessions for the Cheapside project in Lexington, a well-meaning white woman suggested that a tree be planted where the monuments once stood as a way of recognizing the site's egregious history. As she enthusiastically spoke about the life-giving, spiritual, and sentient attributes of trees, I noticed glances exchanged among many of the Black community members in the session. Later, some of these individuals confirmed my suspicion about the cause of the momentary tension—*strange fruit*.

Carmen navigates this tension in her role as chief of staff for a local councilwoman. As part of a municipal initiative to improve air quality and combat an urban heat island—two issues that disproportionately impact Black people in many cities across North America—a fund was created to plant more trees. This would dramatically improve air quality, reduce heat, and provide much-needed respite from Southern sunrays in Black neighbourhoods throughout the city. Despite these public space and health benefits, according to Carmen, many Black community members have been resistant to the initiative.

The formal reason given is a fear of trees falling on their homes or into the streets during a tornado, but Carmen suspects strange fruit is at the core of many residents' concerns. Based on my own experiences in Lexington and beyond, I do too. But how does one begin to talk about how historical and collective trauma lodged deep within the body creates a resistance toward pragmatic public space initiatives like tree planting?

Carmen suggests that a part of the answer is remembering that trees aren't the adversary. She reminds herself of this when she goes RVing in the woods with her parents and siblings. She delights in this indulgence of family time in a beautiful public space, but these getaways are never without a hovering heaviness. The banter between her family and white families also enjoying the outdoors is burdened with a specific kind of small talk, laced with guilt and the ever-present history of the place. And then there is her own internal conflict. Every time she hangs her hammock between two trees, she reminds herself, "Black people and trees are sturdy and have the ability to heal from the harm."

I am struck by the subtle yet powerful correlation she draws between trees and Black bodies. I think about the sacred connection that human beings have with other living beings, particularly sentient beings like trees. Both Black bodies and trees were desecrated by the violence of racial hatred expressed through lynchings. And, like she says, both beings possess the divine attributes of healing. Bodies and trees can fight infection, create healthy physical boundaries, and participate in networks that constitute community. When I think about the reminder Carmen repeats to herself and the correlation she makes between Black bodies and trees, I envisage a symbiotic reclamation of the beauty and inherent sacredness of both beings—branches and Black bodies swaying beneath a blues-filled Southern sky.

–

WHILE ON A site tour in Memphis, I was met by the Mighty Mississippi and reminded of a line in a Langston Hughes poem where he refers to his soul growing deep like the rivers. It was an inexplicable yet undeniable experience of *place attachment*, a key concept in environmental psychology used to describe the emotional bond between people and places. At first, my rational mind tried to explain away the invisible surge between myself and this body of water where Indigenous Americans established both agricultural and urban communities for thousands of years and where, in recent history, African Americans' despair and hope have been lodged in its muddy riverbed. Standing there felt like arriving at a site I'd been summoned to, a site that had been lovingly awaiting my arrival.

Rivers have always been suffused with sacred properties. The Nile River is associated with the mythological god Osiris, linked to the Egyptian creation story, agriculture, and prosperity. Ireland's River Shannon is named after the goddess Sionna, whose name means "possessor of wisdom." The Ganges River is a transboundary body of water associated with the goddess Ganga and revered by Indian Hindus, who believe that scattering the ashes of their dead ensures smooth transition to the next life. The perceived sacredness of these and other rivers is not only connected to mythology and human virtue; they are also held up as hallowed because, in a practical sense, proximity to rivers fosters mobility, prosperity, and food security.

The Mississippi River is paramount in Black people's cultural geography, associated with both oppression and freedom. The river was early America's main transportation artery and carried both cash crops and enslaved African Americans to markets, commerce which is largely responsible for the nation's wealth and many decades as a global superpower. In fact, the phrase "sold down the river," used to describe betrayal or deceitful behaviour, is derived from the practice of packing enslaved African Americans on steamboats, tearing them from their loved ones, and selling them to new enslavers operating cotton and sugar plantations. However, this same body of water was also an escape route for enslaved African Americans in pursuit of a freedom they'd never experienced but knew was owed them.

I felt my ancestors in depths deeper than the Mississippi River itself while standing on her shoreline in Memphis.

Later that afternoon, I delivered a professional development session. Despite having experienced what I can only describe as a *presence*, I guided the session with relative ease and appreciated a congenial exchange between myself, my client partners, and local placemakers. Afterwards, I was approached by a few attendees and invited on neighbourhood walks and for intimate conversation over a meal. And then one local woman suggested that I be introduced to Miss Mary Mitchell, a highly respected local elder, bestowed with the title of honorary historian of Orange Mound by the mayor.

As a small group began to congregate around me, it became clear that Elder Mary's time was not to be played with and, as such, a spontaneous meeting might be a long shot. Also, Elder Mary did not suffer fools, so she obviously didn't have a social media account, and to complicate matters, very few people had her phone number. However, after several calls to distant cousins, a hairdresser, and a not-for-profit developer, it was done. Or almost done. She agreed to meet with me and *then* decide if I would be permitted to walk the sacred grounds of the Orange Mound neighbourhood.

Defiantly founded atop the Deaderick plantation, Orange Mound is recognized as one of the first neighbourhoods conceived and constructed for Black people in the United States. Mary Mitchell was delivered at her Orange Mound home by Jane Thomas, a local midwife, on August 25, 1936. Her parents had four miscarriages before her birth, and despite the jubilation of her arrival, they separated a few years later. She recalls her mother being a stern woman who had lost her own mother at the fragile age of five. A woman who supported but refused to spoil Elder Mary and her siblings. When speaking of her father, Willie Bubba Jones, she says, "Oh God, my dad, my dad . . . was an angel."

As a child, her time was split between her parents, who were uninterested in getting formally divorced, and her paternal grandparents. With the exception of a second-grade scuffle with a light-complected, curly-haired classmate who insisted that she was too good to attend a segregated school with *regular* Black kids, Elder Mary felt loved moving between homes and within the broader community.

When I meet Elder Mary and Elder Luella in a strip mall storefront that has been transformed into a beautiful art gallery and gathering place, I am greeted by the scrutiny of older Black women. Undeterred, I settle into a chair at a small table while the two women ask me about my life in Toronto, experiences as a single mom, and political ideas. I'm a little taken aback by the omission of questions related to my professional practice, but I've come to learn that Black Southerners are pointedly unimpressed; they care more about who your people are, how you occupy space, and your ability to extend respect than your professional credentials.

The conversation is thick with both intimacy and observation, and just as the afternoon succumbs to the evening sky, Elder Mary says, "It's time." By this point it is raining lightly so we decide to navigate the community in a van. Elder Luella, who is the younger of the two women, drives; Elder Mary sits in the front passenger seat; and I quietly take my spot in the back seat, grateful for the journey ahead of us.

Elder Luella drives slowly down a wide road lined with an array of shotgun houses, newer bungalows, and what I can only describe as Southern-style tiny homes. As with most guided tours within Black communities, Elder Mary and Elder Luella begin by talking about the people and culture of the community rather than the striking architecture or impressive amenities. They tell me about luminaries like Dr. Alvin Crawford, the first African American to earn a medical degree from the University of Tennessee, who became internationally acclaimed for orthopedic surgery, and prominent athletes like Tori Noel, who played for the Denver Broncos, and Olympic-gold-medal-winning track athlete Rochelle Stevens. They recall seeing blues legends like B.B. King and Etta James perform, and Elder Mary laughs about this kid Elvis Presley who used to tag along behind local blues musicians and local youth to the Esquire Theatre and W.C. Handy Theatre. They'd joke that he'd better not get 'em in trouble for kidnapping a white boy.

A couple of day workers signal for Elder Luella to lower her window, and they ask her for directions, which leads to a ten-minute conversation about young people these days and the job market. A neighbour wearing bright-coloured gardening gloves leaves her flower bed to help with the directions. When we start driving again, Elder Mary describes the beauty and strong social networks within all Black neighbourhoods.

Although it may seem counterintuitive to most, numerous Black elders who survived Jim Crow segregation have mixed feelings about integration. They critique the ways segregation breached the Constitution by impinging on Black people's social, economic, and physical mobility while underscoring the immense cooperation that existed within segregated Black neighbourhoods.

During segregation, Black people didn't have the luxury of insidious contemporary class divisions. Elder Mary explains, "A doctor had a maid livin' on one side of him and the woman who washed his clothes lived across the street. We couldn't afford to buy into white people's classism nonsense; our very lives depended on mutual respect and cooperation." Although narratives emerging from that era tend to focus on unconscionable marginalization, which is a powerful partial truth, segregated communities were among the first to explicitly practise mutual aid and survived on social capital.

In Orange Mound, Mrs. Springer, Elder Mary's esteemed elementary school principal, walked children home and chatted with their parents. The community was filled with craftsmen who built their homes and paved the sidewalks. Elder Mary's Uncle Salmon had a cleaning business, and he and some other men made and sold bootleg corn liquor. The community made space for everyone.

To punctuate this point, she instructs Elder Luella to drive to a transom house, which was the local space for discreet extramarital affairs and same-sex encounters. The mistress of the house instructed her guests to park a couple of blocks away from the home while she prepared something called a "set up" comprising four glasses, a bowl of ice, liquor, chaser, and three or four quarts of beer. Sometimes you could smell her cooking chitlins in the kitchen, and she always played nice radio music.

She'd also perfectly time appointments so that married couples and church members wouldn't encounter each other while pursuing their sexual interests with individuals in relationships, sex workers, and same-sex love interests. We exit the van, and Elder Mary points out various discreet ways in and out of the house. I can't help but giggle at the subversive place-making and site programming expertise of the woman who ran the home.

Afterwards, knowing that Elder Mary is a woman of faith, I ask her for her views pertaining to same-sex relationships within the neighbourhood, especially a half century ago when damn near everybody was violently homophobic. She says, "We didn't use the correct language back then or speak about homosexuality outright, but we also didn't make anyone feel out of place; we were too busy surviving segregation together."

As we drive to the church, I silently contemplate the issue of homophobia within Black communities, largely steeped in religion. I believe in an omnipotent Creator alongside science and justice, which, for me, are also forms of divinity. Sadly, this must be clarified given the surge of religious fascists preaching hate in the name of an all-loving light of the world.

These and other contradictions complicate my feelings about Christianity, and all organized religions for that matter.

I revere the Black church as an early site of the civil rights and environmental justice movements and for serving as vital communal Black space. However, I also recognize that the church, Black and otherwise, is the site of colonial and patriarchal indoctrination, homophobia, exploitation of poor people, alienation of single mothers, and gross religious capitalism. As we pull up to the Mount Moriah Baptist Church, I put these complications aside to learn about the role of the church in this particular community.

Interestingly, Elder Mary begins by talking about the church as a recreational space for children without the financial means or *right* skin colour to attend summer camps. The church hosted vocational camps where every Black child could participate in organized activities in beautiful green spaces, make art, and develop leadership skills. The children were all provided with lunches and the gear they needed to fully participate in the programming. Each camp ran for a few weeks, so as soon as one was coming to a close, Elder Mary's parents would register her for the next one. This ensured her summers were filled with immense joy.

These local churches transformed into emergency service sites during local crises and served as the NAACP's headquarters, spurring civil rights organizing and, later, other forms of activism. And much like bed and breakfasts provided refuge to early settlers travelling trails and roads across the country, Black churches, along with private homeowners, provided safe accommodations for Black travellers too scared or proud to stay in the city's segregated motels. Elder Mary tells me that to create good Black places, the community must centre "faith, family, and fortitude."

And with that, we set out to our next stop—the park.

Elder Mary and Elder Luella are almost as passionate about their local park as they are about Jesus. "We had so much fun at this park, there wasn't time to worry about why white people didn't want us; they were the ones missing out on what was goin' on with us," says Elder Mary, insisting I get out of the van to really *feel* the place. That's the thing with Black women elders. They don't journey through places; they feel the spirit of places, with tissues and Bible verses tucked in their brassieres. Elder Mary doesn't mess with Google Maps; she charts her daily routes based on her gut and her God. And while I've been colonized out of these ancestral instincts, I step out of the van and try to deeply feel the ground, now moist from the evening rain, beneath my feet.

The pair excitedly speak over each other, pointing out where Black people played tennis and golf. There was also a baseball diamond where Black softball teams would fiercely compete and an area where Black families would elevate the hot-dog picnic to epic cookouts complete with sweet corn and just the right amount of char on barbecue ribs to convert vegetarians to meat eaters. Close by, there used to be a swimming pool where the local youth received Red Cross certification and sometimes the church choir came calling blessings down from heaven before mass baptisms in the pool.

They weren't the only ones who enlivened the street adjacent to the park with music. A kid named Charles Lloyd serenaded parkgoers with saxophone solos. He grew up to become a celebrated jazz musician sharing stages with jazz greats like Charles Mingus, and while practising transcendental meditation in the 1970s, he performed extensively with the Beach Boys.

Before we head back to the van, we pause for a moment, and, in a sombre voice, Elder Mary says, "Over there is where the master's mansion used to be." Once again, I feel the presence I'd encountered earlier at the river and wonder if, like my Black elders, I am becoming a woman who *feels* spaces and places.

The light evening drizzle turns to rain, and Elder Luella suggests that we speak more about the plantation site from the van while driving to the home of the late T.O. Jones, a sanitation worker who became a formidable union organizer after the gruesome deaths of Echol Cole and Robert Walker, who were killed by state negligence in one of many malfunctioning municipal garbage trucks. On February 1, 1968, also a rainy day, the two young men reported for their shift. Much like us, they sought refuge in a vehicle, in their case the back of the garbage truck they worked on. Tragically, there was no refuge to be found. A malfunctioning motor triggered the truck's compactor and both men were crushed alive.

The City of Memphis extended a mere five hundred dollars for funeral expenses and one month's pay for each man. This meagre compensation was bolstered by a $100,000 contribution from Black Memphians and an additional $25,000 from the United Auto Workers. Despite these charitable community contributions, many rightfully remained dissatisfied with the municipality's response to the families directly impacted by the tragedy and to the workers more broadly.

T.O. Jones, a fellow sanitation worker and union leader, galvanized members of the Public Works Department to fight for better safety standards and decent wages for Black workers. Local students of all races and Black church leaders marched alongside the Black sanitation workers. Their nonviolent protest was met with police brutality but protestors were unrelenting. The movement caught fire and the attention of Dr. Martin Luther King Jr.

King arrived in Memphis, and, in front of an unprecedented indoor crowd of over 25,000 civil rights protestors, commended the sanitation workers and the city for showing solidarity. He encouraged everyone to support a city-wide work stoppage and pledged to return a few days later. He kept his word, but when violence and chaos erupted during the march, he was whisked away and there was disagreement as to whether or not he should return to support the movement.

He returned on April 3 and wearily addressed a crowd, contemplating his own mortality: "I've seen the Promised Land. I may not get there with you. But I want you to know tonight that we, as a people, will get to the Promised Land." His words were prophetic. The following evening, while preparing for dinner, Dr. Martin Luther King Jr. was assassinated while standing on the balcony of the Lorraine Motel. And somehow, I was now standing in front of the home of T.O. Jones, the union organizer who compelled him to come to Memphis.

I'd read the story of Dr. King's death so many times. The day before my walk in Orange Mound, I had even visited the room where Dr. King stayed before he was assassinated. But I'd never heard it described with such intimacy. I share my awe, and Elder Luella casually says, "Chile, I'm the mama of two of T.O. Jones's babies so I know an extra thing or two about this story." I silently say a prayer for T.O. Jones and Dr. King as I stand at the entrance of a boarded-up home that should, instead, be a heritage site, paying homage to a local hero who helped to shape the city's and country's history. I'm overwhelmed by the privilege of literally walking in T.O. Jones's footsteps.

Nightfall creeps up on us. Elder Mary announces that she's added one more stop to the neighbourhood tour, her family home. This is the moment I knew she'd become my forever elder. Elder Luella cautiously navigates low-lit roads slick from rain until we arrive at a modest, well-kept single-family home with the porch light on. "This is where I learned faith, family, and fortitude," says Elder Mary.

Despite being a child of divorce, her intergenerational home was never *broken*. Elder Mary's grandmother was an avid reader and nurtured her love of books. Her uncles frequently visited with sweets and raucous stories. Sometimes her aunt, a head maid who raised four generations of "good white folks," took her to visit her employer in a red construction truck. One summer when Mary was twelve or so, she got a babysitting job with that same family and presumed to enter through the front door, disrupting a tea party, and "almost caught a whipping." One of the women lunged at her, shrieking, "You little pickaninny." Mary dropped to the ground and escaped through the narrow opening between the woman's plump legs and out on to the streets. "I had no idea that people who looked like me were supposed to use the back door because in this house right here," she says, gesturing to her childhood home, "we were loved and taught that we had value."

This seeded a sense of love and value crucial to helping Elder Mary navigate an unplanned pregnancy at the age of fifteen. Despite her good grades, the school immediately retracted her recommendation to join the honour society and pressured her to withdraw from her classes. Mary refused: "The last thing my baby needed was an empty-headed mama." Her family supported her decision to stay and so she walked the hallways, head held high, deflecting speculative stares, until her water broke.

Shortly after her son, Larry Elton Jones, was born, her daddy, Willie Bubba Jones, came around with a bag full of pink baby clothes because the family had been certain that she would give birth to a girl. But Willie Bubba Jones didn't miss a step. He proudly dressed Larry in an all-pink outfit, wrapped him in unconditional love, and walked—slightly pigeon-toed—to the street corner to show off his first grandson.

Mary returned to school to earn her GED and went on to become one of the first Black directors of medical records in the state. During her tenure working at the hospital, she was warned to stand at a distance from patients and clients: "It was as though these people thought my Black could rub off on 'em." She was often mistaken for restaurant or cleaning staff and was always eager to clear up any confusion. In 1968, Elder Mary helped to integrate the institution's dining room by simply refusing to eat elsewhere.

She left that job to expand her family and sell women's accessories with a close friend. Their business was one of three African American businesses granted a lease for space in the airport at the time. Although Elder Mary's aptitude and ambition helped take her farther than her teachers and a few other naysayers imagined when she became pregnant, she always remained rooted in Orange Mound.

Both Elder Mary and Elder Luella have contributed to the lifeblood of the community. They've led initiatives related to public space stewardship, crime prevention, and cultural heritage preservation. The mayor named Elder Mary the community's honorary historian, and Congressman Steve Cohen wrote a letter about her commitment to the community that is currently registered in the Hall of Records. By the end of our Orange Mound tour, I realize Elder Mary's love for this community, a community built by Black labour and audacious Black hope atop sorrow-soaked soil, is sacred. And that was why I had to be carefully vetted before being permitted entry.

–

MANY BLACK DETROITERS will tell you that all of Detroit is sacred, not as hyperbole but as holy declaration. I believe them, and I believe in them. I think their sense of sacred space is largely rooted in the Great Migration, a pathway to the promised land travelled from 1916 to 1970. Millions of Black Americans unwedged themselves from under Jim Crow's boot to search for access to education, economic opportunities, and freedom from racial violence in the Midwest, West, and *ever-hallowed* North. As these migrants journeyed toward what was once America's wealthiest municipality, I imagine many thought they were about to walk upon what the Book of Revelation describes as the pure gold streets of the great city.

As with most waypoints of migration, the train station is often imbued with the spiritual virtues and idealism of arrival sites such as inner peace and hope for an unknown future. And like most train stations, Michigan Central Station holds a layered and significant history for many Detroiters, including those who sought freedom from the oppressive segregation of the South.

Michigan Central is at once grand and ordinary amid Detroit's enviable architectural landscape. Located in the Corktown neighbourhood, the station was designed by the lauded architects of New York City's Grand Central Station. Modelled after an ancient Roman bathhouse, the station was admired for its vaulted ceilings and lavish bronze chandeliers, which presided over luxe marble floors. It was also a functional and pragmatic place, serving as the region's primary transportation depot from the early 1900s to the late 1980s.

As modes of movement shifted and there was a sharp decline in rail travel in favour of automobile and air travel, ridership numbers plummeted, and the station was shuttered in the winter of 1988. For the following three decades, this once renowned transportation hub sat dormant, diminished to a popular subject of ruins photography, laying the building's barbed wire and broken glass bare.

In 2018, the Ford Motor Company purchased the building with aspirations of building a thirty-acre innovation hub. Its doors opened to a mixture of sentimentality and sharp critique; there were concerns that an innovation hub did not reflect the presence or priorities of Black Detroiters.

Nathaniel Wallace—a highly regarded suit-and-tie guy with an undeniable hint of 'hood swagger—is quite literally navigating these disparate place-based perceptions on a daily basis. As the head of civic partnerships for Ford, Nathaniel and his team work at the intersection of arts, tech, and community engagement. Nathaniel works out of the Book Depository Building across the street from the station. Both the tensions and opportunities inherent in his team's portfolio coalesce on the community level.

He encounters community members who share in collective place-based memory informed by both social structures and the built environment. One afternoon, a Black woman who appeared to be in her mid-sixties walked into the Grand Hall with a little girl. Suddenly, the elder woman erupted in tears. Not wanting to disturb the sanctity of the moment, Nathaniel stood back and bore witness as the woman looked down at her granddaughter and said, "Here is where I met my father, your great-granddaddy. He looked so mean, and soon as he saw me, he had the biggest smile."

Not all the stories associated with the station are heartwarming. He once encountered another woman weeping, this one younger. Her tears were not infused with sentimentality and joy. She said that the grandeur of the building reminded her of the Catholic church. She associated standing in Michigan Central with the smallness and repression she felt as a result of religious doctrine.

While Nathaniel doesn't often refer to Michigan Central or other places in Detroit as sacred, due to the potential conflation of the word with organized religion, he acknowledges that the relationship between Black Detroiters and public spaces extends beyond the natural realm. Pointing to the "Detroit vs. Everybody" slogan as their defiant version of "I Love New York," he explains how Black Detroiters maintained a sense of faith in their city even while struggling through the municipality's bankruptcy, loss of homes, outmigration, and the state's neglect of its public spaces. Rather than succumbing to shame and the national narrative about the city's demise, they maintained what their churchgoing elders would refer to as "hope in things not seen."

The resurrection of Michigan Central Station, and the potential to breathe new life into the site, may well contribute to the miracle that is Detroit.

–

LAUREN HOOD, A reputable community development expert and researcher, tells me that she felt "divinely ordered" to purchase the Metropolitan Community Tabernacle church, which she is in the process of transforming into a futuristic Black public space. In addition to being a visionary, Lauren is unapologetically *woo-woo*. Her entire retelling of how she—well, actually, her organization, the Institute for AfroUrbanism—came to acquire the church is predicated on vibes and a series of so-called coincidences.

One afternoon, while driving through the north end of the city, Lauren felt a spiritual pull toward the property. A little less than 4,000 square feet, the building was modestly sized with worn but warm brick, and, although completely gutted, it had the most attractive set of sturdy bones. In addition to the building's solid construction, the perimeter of the property caught Lauren's attention: "Its condition was well-preserved in comparison to the adjacent properties, and the newly constructed fenceline gave me the sense that it was protected." Upon making inquiries about the property, she learned that the owner was a friend. Two other offers, one of them cash and another from big business, were made, but Lauren never feared losing out on her opportunity to purchase the property. As anticipated, within a year and a half, Lauren had successfully purchased the property for her new development, christened Dreamstead.

While Lauren is not conventionally religious, she recognizes the important placemaking function of the Black church in Detroit. Historically, the Black church has been a site of political organizing, mutual aid, and crisis response. Uninterested in fire-and-brimstone sermons—"I don't do strife and scarcity"—she is interested in having a Sunday service of sorts where the community can come and be spiritually fed. Reflecting on the divergent experiences of her eighty-eight-year-old mother, who is fairly socially isolated in the absence of a "church family," and her ninety-three-year-old aunt, who maintains an active public life because of her connection to the church, Lauren emphasizes the continued connection between church and community.

Lauren is also moved by the church's connection to the broader neighbourhood and its history. Dubbed the North End, residents here experienced a cultural and economic upsurge in the early 1900s with the success of the automotive industry. Motown musical icons like Diana Ross and Aretha Franklin came from the North End, and it is said to be the birthplace of techno music. It is also one of communities where a large number of residents, displaced from the Black Bottom and Paradise Valley neighbourhoods due to the construction of one of the America's first depressed highways, found home. Constructed during the mid-twentieth century's "urban renewal" era, the highway erased beautiful homes, thriving businesses, community services, and entertainment spaces.

For Lauren, the fact that the church endured during a time when Black Detroiters who had suffered this brutal blow to their sense of place found sanctuary in the North End affirms her sense that the site holds sacred properties. Established in 1922, the church was fully paid for and built by the hands of its congregation. From the beginning, a powerful pride of place and sense of agency permeated throughout its congregation. Old newspaper clippings tell a story of fellowship suppers and interracial Bible conferences. Although the church closed its doors in the mid-nineties, its spirit of community and local power prevailed. Lauren was immediately compelled to build on this legacy. That said, her aspirations transcend the bounds of reconciling the past, the sense of community created in church pews, and even Detroit itself. She imagines her redeveloped church and its property serving as a cultural hub for Black people around the globe.

She isn't simply striving for a safe and well-maintained space for Black communities. "This should be a given," she says. Lauren wants to create a space where Black people are not grateful for these basics but rather can encounter healing and true self-actualization. A space imaginative and just enough to hold the multitudes of Black people's future selves—both tangible and metaphysical.

And while her influences are primarily derived from these aspirations, inherent to Black futurism, she also draws broader inspiration from what she refers to as Europe's "cultural vibrations." Once, when she ordered an espresso to go, the barista asked where she was in a rush to get to, perplexed that she wasn't going to pause in place and savour her hot drink. This, too, has shaped her sense of the sacred.

One summer, Lauren invited me to visit her new development. While viewing the glorious external green space dotted with minimalistic black picnic benches—lovingly stewarded by Audra Carson, a beautification and sustainability strategist—the skies began to weep with joy.

We quickly ran into the belly of Lauren's partially gutted church. "I'm inspired by how the Harlem Renaissance was seeded by a dinner party," she says, slightly damp and breathless. "So, I imagine a big table anchoring the space, which could be used for meal sharing and panel discussions 'cause you know how we love food." Amid our laughter and Lauren's dreaming aloud, I learn that she wants to ensure that the spaces within and outside the church are multi-use and have a fluid feel, which precludes things like furniture being nailed to the floor or restrictive rules limiting imagination.

Gesturing back to the green space, which was alive and glistening with rain, she says, "I want to have a garden with healing herbs and produce that we can cook in here . . . Yes, there must be a kitchen . . ." It was as though she was creating the space in real time, weaving together words like a builder pouring concrete to fortify her dream's foundation.

-

A FEW YEARS ago, Orlando Bailey, a young Emmy Award–winning journalist credited with shaping not only some of Detroit's most important narratives but public spaces themselves through his community engagement, shared a personal story with me that has since clung to my core. It's not a story about a historically mammoth site like Michigan Central or the reclamation of a small culturally significant site like Dreamstead. Orlando's Detroit sacred space story is about the development of a strip mall.

Yes, a strip mall.

Orlando's grandmother, Mamie Adams, was born in the Mississippi Delta, a region so poor it's been described as a third world country in the heart of America. By the 1940s, she and her two siblings and grandparents left a place so small that, according to Orlando, "you won't find it on a map." After settling in Detroit, her grandparents were able to purchase a home, where she helped to raise her nine siblings, the youngest of whom still resides in their intergenerational family home.

"My grandmother's home, which she owned, was in many ways a public space; she opened her doors to help those who needed a bit of time to get on their feet and for community gatherings," Orlando says. On any given weekend, neighbours would come around to discuss local politics and share stories. Orlando delighted in his grandmother allowing him "to be in grown folks' business" a little longer than the other children and credits time spent in these adult circles with helping to create a sense of community awareness and accountability early in his life. This blurring between domestic and public space is common in Black communities.

This distinct phenomenon is partially rooted in Black people's cultural values. The home is not a nuclear family space but an intergenerational space and an extension of the village. It's also a pragmatic response to segregation, racist public space policies, and social attitudes, which either prohibited Black people from gathering in plain sight or made it dangerous for them to do so. Orlando's grandmother, like so many of our Black elders, blurred the boundaries of domestic and public space as a form of Black placemaking and preservation of Black people's sacred infrastructure.

Over the years, witnessing and contributing to Detroit's transformation, Orlando has developed a special appreciation for his grandmother's home, particularly its large living room, as a semi-public space. Colourful fabric throws were carefully arranged across a sectional that created ample seating for small group gatherings. As in most Black people's living rooms back in the 1970s and '80s, framed Jesus hands presided over the space along with a plaque of the poem "Footprints in the Sand" to remind guests of His ever-present care.

One thing Mamie Adams loved almost as much as her community was thrifting. Her living room was filled with artwork and quirkier items such as a pair of lamps that had women's bodies as the base. Her most famous find was a glass table held up by a curvaceous and detailed mermaid. Dubbed the "mermaid table," this centrepiece, which Orlando's grandmother spray-painted to match her updated decor over the years, captured her spunky and bold personality.

"It makes me emotional when I think about having the honour of growing up in a sacred space that my grandmother created. Long before urbanists coined the term *placemaking*, my grandmother was modelling this for me," Orlando says.

The moment that marked her home as sacred for him as a young man occurred in the early 2000s. Mamie Adams stood strong in her communal living room not with the community members she had lovingly created space for over the years but with developers seeking to purchase her home to construct a strip mall on the Lower Eastside of the city. She was the last holdout, surrounded by empty lots that had previously been her neighbours' homes, and the developer needed her to sell. Orlando was a freshman in high school, and it was the first time he'd seen white people in his grandmother's home.

He watched as his grandmother asserted her power, knowing exactly what the land and home were worth, both monetarily and to the community. She negotiated a fair price for the home, a challenging feat for many Black people when confronted by developers and a technocratic system that once positioned their very bodies as property. At the end of the meeting, one of the developers asked, "Can we help you with anything else?" And like lightning, this audacious matriarch responded, "Yes, you can help me move."

Orlando and I always laugh at this point in the story. While allowances for moving were likely embedded in the agreement, his grandmother needed those men to know that there were no limits to what she felt she and her broader community deserved.

I think about how his grandmother's example and his early exposure to sacred space shaped the way he showed up for me when my partner was attacked at the height of COVID-19. I'd been invited to my alma mater to develop and teach a now award-winning course focused on Black placemakers across North America. As one of the featured experts studied in the course, Orlando was at the online launch of the published case studies.

What he and the hundreds of online attendees didn't know was that the night before the launch, my partner, a Filipino Canadian man, had been threatened by a young white man wielding hate speech and a knife. Anti-Asian hate has spiked on both sides of the border due to dangerous political rhetoric. Thanks to my partner's immense composure and the courage of passersby, the perpetrator was apprehended by police. But I'd been awake all night contemplating the cancellation of the launch.

A few minutes into the formal launch presentation, I heard myself say, "I'm a kid from the 'hood . . ." In that moment, I knew that I was going to betray everything I'd learned about performing *well* in public, but I didn't know what would happen next. Through tears, I shared what had taken place the day before, highlighting the importance of us all being each other's "most safe and sacred space."

Orlando turned on his camera and extended his hand and support through the screen. "I want to honour you, Jay Pitter, as my friend, family, and big sister." The Zoom chat was immediately flooded with comments:

"I was asked to come here as a work assignment, and it ended up being the most spiritually awakening experience I have had the pleasure to be a part of . . ."

"So moving. Thank you for the holy tears . . . for the blessing of bringing your hearts and souls to this essential and inspiring work."

"Didn't know I was coming to church today, but my soul is so glad I did."

Although we were all online, I could quite literally feel Orlando's hand in mine. His words transformed the space for me and hundreds of attendees behind our digital devices. Somewhere on the east side of Detroit, a small section of a strip mall used to be the living room of a woman from a place so small it can't be found on a map—a woman named Mamie Adams who taught my friend Orlando Bailey how to create sacred space.

-

WHEN I THINK about spaces like Orlando's grandmother's living room, now a part of a strip mall, a powerful placemaking quote comes to mind. Author and environmental activist Wendell Berry once said, "There are no unsacred places; there are only sacred places and desecrated places." In addition to affirming the sanctity of all creation, his observation makes me reflect on how limiting the idea is that places of worship or pilgrimage routes are the only sacred sites. Our actions, intentions, and connections within a space are what truly imbues them with sacredness. All spaces and places have a spirit or intangible character of some kind.

Within traditional African and broader cultural contexts, the spirit of a place refers to an intangible, often inexpressible sense one gets based on an ancestral presence, natural environment, rituals, and the energy emanating from people. This sense or spirit of a place is often referred to as the vibe in Black culture. While we didn't create the term per se, we popularized it through publications like *Vibe*—a magazine co-launched by Quincy Jones in the early 1990s— and terms like *vibe check*—sometimes used as a type of cultural place-based audit—or *good vibes only*—a way of summoning support in the face of systemic oppression—or referring to someone as *a whole vibe*—high praise for dope style and character.

Since the kids are constantly evolving the use of this and other terms, I consult with my mentee, Selma Elkhazin, a gifted cultural planner. "When my peers and I say something is such a vibe, we're not trying to start an intellectual conversation about metaphysical aspects of intangible cultural heritage," she explains. "What we're saying more specifically is that my spirit feels culturally connected to the spirit of this place."

According to Selma, whose viewpoints I take on good authority, elements that create a vibe within the Black spaces she frequents give an immediate sense of belonging and being "let in on a cultural secret" the moment she's crossed the threshold of a public space. A vibe can be very chill or really hype. What's key is people being true to themselves, which "can mean dancing in a circle with a crowd of people cheering and cooling you off with splashes of their bottled water, or it can mean taking everything in with a friend from a distance along the wall," she explains.

Also, competition and putting on social airs kill the vibe. "For a young woman, one of the things that makes a place a vibe is sisterhood, like girls who don't know each other fixing each other's lashes in the bathroom or sharing their brand of lip gloss," she tells me. The people in the space contribute to the vibe, so being present is also important. "If everyone is on their phone, there's definitely not a vibe; the vibe is created through presence and participation . . . It's a synergy between the individual, the group of people, and the place."

Regardless of our generational differences, and the term evolving into new phrases and hashtags, the vibe Selma describes is underpinned by the same values and insider experiences I experienced at her age. At the same time, our understanding of the vibe, or spirit, of a place isn't entirely culturally specific. Just as public spaces are universal, so is our ability to feel their intangible, mystical energy. This feeling between two or more people of any identity, who value the space and each other, is central to the consecration of public spaces.

–

THE DAP, WHICH is an acronym for dignity and pride, dates back to Black service members fighting in Vietnam. This hand and body gesture conveyed solidarity, survival, and mutual care during international war and domestic discrimination. African American photographer and visual artist LaMont Hamilton conducted watershed research on the history of the dap, beautifully documenting its countless creative variations.

However, like many Black public space rituals, it has been popularized and separated from its origin story.

However, the dap is no less sacred or culturally significant than the namaste greeting originating from India—a *mudra* (gesture) of upward-pointing, pressed-together palms meaning "I bow to and see the divine in you"—or the Māori *hongi* greeting—a ritual where two people press their foreheads and noses together to signify sharing the same breath of life. Despite becoming a popular gesture, like other deeply meaningful greeting rituals, the dap also merits reverence.

-

THE MORNING I was scheduled to deliver a keynote on place, joy, and justice at Cornell University, I was nervous. It was during the uncertainty of the pandemic, and, for the first time, I'd be delivering a keynote wearing a mask. My tonsils were slightly inflamed, a clear sign of nervousness. My family doctor once told me that because communication was so central to who I was, I didn't experience nervousness or other types of emotional discomfort in my gut like most people, I held it in my tonsils. She told me that removing them would be removing a built-in emotional thermometer tracking my communicative and overall wellness. She encouraged me to reflect on any communication challenges I might be having, both personally and professionally, at the onset of irritation, and, instead of treating the symptom, I could address the source—the communication challenge. My inflamed tonsils, not butterflies in my stomach, were how I knew I was nervous.

The kind woman at the Cornell front desk also knew I was nervous. She suggested I take a moment to have an herbal tea in an upper lounge. As I was walking toward the stairs, I heard her call upstairs and say, "I've sent Jay, one of our keynote speakers, up to you for an herbal tea. Please ensure she's comfortable."

The moment I approached the entrance, a tall gentleman whom I assumed was the maître d' greeted me by name. As he was inquiring if I was interested in breakfast, I spotted one of the foremost African American philosophers and public intellectuals across the room: Cornel West. The irony of being at Cornell University in a lounge with Cornel West was and is too weird to process.

Partially because I genuinely didn't want to be intrusive and because I was nervous, I asked the host if he thought it would be okay for me to stop by Mr. West's table to briefly greet him. As he was indicating it would be okay, Cornel West got up from his table, likely noticing the way I was looking at him without blinking, and started walking toward me. Both the host and I froze.

"It's so good to meet you," he said. *So good to meet me?* He went on to chat with me like we were neighbours who frequently bumped into each other at the local coffee shop or bus stop. I somehow managed to get out a few coherent words of appreciation for his ideas and told him how they helped shape aspects of my placemaking practice. He listened to every word I said with his entire body and never once stopped smiling. Noticing my phone, he asked, "Can we get a photo together?"

In that Ivy League lounge, Cornel West greeted me in a way that, similar to the dap, conveyed solidarity and care, transforming the luxe rug beneath both our feet into sacred ground.

–

TWO DECADES EARLIER, on a very different campus across the country, Tamika Butler was also sanctifying the ground. When she first tells me that she is a "Black Greek," I think, "How did I not know Tamika was biracial?" I spend a lot of time in the U.S., but I'm Canadian, and Black fraternities and sororities are less prevalent here. As Tamika further describes how she became a Black Greek, I chuckle at my initial misunderstanding and catch up. "My older sister was a Greek at the University of Nebraska–Lincoln but I never thought I'd become a Greek," she says.

Tamika's thoughts about joining the fraternity changed when she started attending Creighton University, also in Nebraska, in 2002. It was a Jesuit school, with a predominantly white student body. The few Black students on campus found their footing participating in the Black Student Union and events organized by Black fraternities. Because the Black population in Omaha was also small, Black Greeks from multiple campuses in the region combined their efforts when carrying out community service or throwing parties.

There wasn't a single eureka moment or monumental shift that brought Tamika into the fraternity. It was experiencing the group's collaborative spirit by attending events like basketball games and contributing to their fundraisers and other initiatives like Girls Inc. Day. The group didn't have a house, nor were they caught up in the hazing and elite culture that, in some instances, permeates similar groups. "After hanging out with folks I just kinda vibed with at social and service events, I decided to join," she says.

As a young, politically aware Black woman who wasn't into guys, the whole Catholic school thing didn't really fit, but Tamika found a special place among the "Divine Nine," which refers to historically African American Greek-letter fraternities and sororities. Soon she found herself driving miles to go to step dance competitions—a dynamic dance rooted in the

South African gumboot genre and military drills that have been reinterpreted by Black fraternities to convey community and kinship. On campus, they held daily communion on the stairs inside of the student centre or outside on the benches: "We didn't need directions like head towards the such-and-such kiosk and turn right. It was understood exactly which places had been blessed as Black Greek sacred sites." These were the places where they "peacocked," as Tamika calls it, and flirted, and where they found refuge in each other when a professor said something that made them feel diminished in class. This is where they did their homework together and collectively dreamt aloud. This is where, on a mostly white campus, when they saw each other, one would call out "Zi Fi," and, without the slightest hesitation, another would answer "so sweet."

Aside from the unyielding support of her family, these rituals, which transformed the Catholic campus into a culturally sanctified space, are where Tamika found the affirmation to successfully move on to Stanford Law School, and to UCLA's Luskin School of Public Affairs, where she is currently an urban planning doctoral student. To this day, there is a particular ritual, the stroll, which she holds with great sentimentality.

Conceived in the early 1900s, the stroll is a unified public space procession, which sometimes includes clapping and call and response, emerging from West and Central African oral and liturgical traditions. Distinguished historian Sterling Stuckey wrote that the call and response "functioned as an insurgent form of belonging and resistance." When Tamika and other Black Greeks linked their arms together in the stroll, the ground immediately became imbued with cultural sacredness that they insisted be respected. Understanding the symbolism of the stroll, they also recognized the stroll of other fraternities. "If I was with my white friends and they tried to cut through a stroll, I'd say, 'Nah, Sally, let's walk around,'" Tamika says. Sometimes the stroll meant that students would have to take a slightly longer route to class but Tamika didn't care. The ground she and other Black Greeks were strolling on was, in that moment, hallowed, and they absolutely refused to unlink their arms.

PART FIVE

JOY

In 2024, as I prepared to receive the Harry Jerome Leadership Award, the third formal recognition for my practice's contributions within a six-month period, I couldn't help but think of Pamela Elizabeth. As I glanced over at my dress and custom-made matching headpiece hanging in the closet—both a hopeful shade of yellow—I felt a surge of gratitude for my mother, now a near stranger. Somewhere within the woman with a chosen name that never quite fit and whose public space rules demanded *perfect performance*, there was a well-meaning mother who dared me to "pass my place." As I applied almond oil to my body and a lip mask in preparation for the evening, I felt a complicated yet warranted sense of gratitude.

When I arrived at the venue, I quickly acknowledged my group of friends, expectantly huddled at the entrance. An event greeter led me away for red carpet interviews. My favourite interviewers were two little girls, approximately six and ten years old, practising their journalism skills with their parents encouraging them on the other side of the velvet rope. After answering several similarly worded questions about my key public space inspirations from the adult journalists, there was a last call in the VIP lounge. Quickly catching the attention of my crew, patiently waiting off to the side, we headed to the lounge to snack on fancy hors d'oeuvres like a bunch of teenagers let loose in the big city with fake IDs on a Saturday night.

In the main hall, as my bio was read aloud, a video montage featuring my daughter, Kirsten—to whom I'd dedicated the honour—was played. Between the parental pride and the liberation that perhaps comes with being a fifty-something woman, when it was time for me to accept the award, the risk of going off script increased exponentially with each step I took toward the podium.

I began by talking about how my greatest honour was being Kirsten's mother and mentioned that she, too, had recently won an award—referring to the Juno (the Canadian equivalent of a Grammy) that she'd won for her first electronic album.

As I looked out into the audience, filled with dignitaries and the professional elite, I felt compelled to recognize the people whose shoulders we all stood upon, who were almost always excluded from formal spaces of celebration. Thinking of my own grandmother, a gifted seamstress who scrubbed floors so my family could immigrate to Canada from Jamaica, I said, "This award is for the domestic workers and the aunties without the luxury of leisure and privilege to dress up stush [the Jamaican term for bougie] in these rooms."

My table of friends rose to their feet, egging me on in the way that only a handful of people who know my childhood story, and what my longtime friend Lance refers to as my "secret raucous laugh," would. The sheer freedom I felt had me transitioning from my professional speaking style to 1980s hip hop shoutouts. "Shout out to the baby mamas, the public housing kids . . ." This electrified dozens of guests in the room who, moments before, had been nestled at their assigned tables, helmed in by protocol and high-quality shapewear beneath their expensive sequined gowns. I beamed as they moved toward the stage in a chorus of amens and what felt like choreographed nods.

As I left the stage, I wondered what many Black people and women who are truly themselves in public wonder: "Was I a bit too much?" My doubt was immediately disrupted by a lineup of guests who shared with me how seen and included my speech had made them feel.

A young single mom told me that she had two children at home and often felt ashamed in these spaces. Learning that

I was once a young single mom with audacious aspirations made her feel like she belonged.

A small group of professionals who came from working-class backgrounds thanked me for acknowledging their parents, whose calloused hands cleared a path wide enough for their education and dreams.

Best of all, two people from the public housing community where I grew up thanked me for "reppin' our block" and remaining real in a situation that demanded a certain level of self-erasure.

Back at my table, I jokingly admonished my friends for egging me on, and I was met with an unapologetic play-by-play of their favourite parts of my irreverent acceptance speech. The six or so of us able to keep our eyes open past ten o'clock, which admittedly usually doesn't include me, decided to meet up at an impromptu afterparty at Daniel and Ty's downtown condominium.

Curled up on the couch of their mid-century modern living room, nibbling on snacks, flanked by an enviable art and book collection, their cat, Daphne, snuggled up to me in an effort to snag the canary-yellow feathers from my headpiece. Her endless pursuit prompted bursts of laughter between talk that wasn't so much small as it was light.

In the afterglow of public joy, I contemplated what had taken place earlier that evening. Despite the overwhelmingly positive feedback, the little girl taught perfect performance could not help but consider how a handful of guests and organizers had averted eye contact. It was as though I'd betrayed the silent yet powerfully salient rules of the space. And worse, I'd done so on purpose.

Surely someone who delivered keynotes to hundreds of mayors and to UN Women about public spaces both understands and has followed formal protocols on dozens of occasions. Risking rumination, I forced myself back into my body and the warm embrace of my friends in the room. While I, like everyone else, yearn for the safety and benefits of performing well in public, there is no award that could foster greater joy than choosing myself and the people who value me above any external gaze.

–

TO UNDERSTAND THE concept of Black public joy, or public joy of any kind, it's imperative to first begin by defining or at least exploring the dimensions of joy itself. *The Journal of Positive Psychology*, among other writings on the subject, points out how this topic has been overlooked: "Joy has been one of the least studied human emotions despite the fact that it is on everyone's list of basic or primary emotions."

Often mistakenly conflated with happiness—by both people and dictionaries—joy has a number of complex distinctions and dimensions. "The two are fairly distinct, according to most researchers," says Matt Sosnowsky, a Philadelphia-based psychotherapist. He explains that happiness tends to be situational and momentary, while joy is a more enduring emotion. Others studying the theory and science of joy believe that it is more than an emotion. It is often described as a state of mind of consistent contentment with life born out of resilience, gratitude, and a sense of belonging.

Some experts focus on community as the nucleus of joy, citing the importance of places like parks, cultural events, and walkable communities that facilitate human-scale connection. Other experts focus on the brain and study the ways dopamine, serotonin, and endorphins are activated during particular experiences. The framing and findings of joy research often overlap. For example, brain chemicals that produce what would be considered positive emotions are often activated when people are riding their bikes in protected lanes or sharing a meal in a communal space. These and similar activities also build a sense of belonging and gratitude.

Just as the focal points of joy research are not entirely mutually exclusive, neither are notions of joy and happiness. Both can exist in a single moment, and some researchers reference happiness when exploring joy. Like many words, the constructs of both *happiness* and *joy* are open to cultural, situational, and structural interpretations. What's most striking to me is the positioning of joy as more than a fleeting emotion wholly dependent on external and environmental stimuli.

Happiness, however elusive, has been our preferred pursuit, perhaps because we are implicitly socialized to seek emotions considered positive outside of ourselves. Establishing and maintaining *a joyful way of being* amid the turbulence of life is a far less attractive proposition given the immense amount of labour required, both as individuals and in the constant making and remaking of community.

When contemplating concepts that, if we're honest, defy language, I turn to some of our greatest thinkers—poets. Beloved Black feminist scholar Audre Lorde spoke of sharing joy as a way to build bridges across our differences. She also referenced learning "how to take joy in all the people I am," which affirms our personal pluralism or, more simply said, various aspects of our ever-changing selves.

Elizabeth Mudenyo, a brilliant young next-generation poet from the part of Toronto where I grew up, writes about "taking joy with both hands" and "making a practice of calling joy into our lives," which for me suggests an active co-creation of joy.

I am convinced that the poetry of grasping and making joy into a life practice across the places and stages of our lives is at the core of creating consistent contentment.

Consistent contentment would, as pointed out by experts, exist alongside challenging emotions. In a book of essays titled *Inciting Joy*, *New York Times*–bestselling author Ross Gay, who is a founding board member of a nonprofit food justice and joy project that advocates for free fruit for all, affirms this contradiction. He asks, "What if joy and pain are fundamentally tangled up with one another?"

Although less than ideal or fair, the notion that joy and pain can occur concurrently particularly resonates for me when thinking about public places. All public spaces hold what educator and researcher Herleen Arora describes as a "poetic tension." From one perspective, public spaces hold histories of colonial atrocity, land-based oppression, physical inaccessibility, and gender-based violence. From another perspective, public spaces hold immense possibility, beauty, and connection. These two opposing forces are always operating amid the cultivation and expression of joy. When I think about public joy, Black or otherwise, I imagine all of these strands, all of our hurts and aspirations, entangled together.

–

BODIES ARE PLACES, assumed sovereign states with fleshy constitutions made vulnerable by political projections. They are naked landscapes of blood, breached borders, and fractured memory. However fragile and prone to judgment, bodies, across various degrees of physical ability, are capable of adapting and healing. Like a park or library, bodies are sites able to redefine themselves. If war can be waged against Black and other exploited bodies, then what prevents those bodies from being reclaimed by individuals as sites for waging joy?

Much has been written about the various fashion statements linked to Black political movements. During the civil rights movement, many activists wore formal, mainstream attire such as suits and ties and crisp A-line skirts, which some observers claim was in part a way of convincing white institutions to embrace integration.

Later, during the Black Panther movement, this "respectable attire" was replaced with leather jackets, dashikis, and voluminous Afros beneath berets. This style statement was counter-cultural and intended to convey militance. Both the Black Power and Black is Beautiful eras pivoted the style of the Black individual and communities in an effort to uplift distinct cultural identities and our own interdependence.

In more recent times, many Black women and 2SLGBTQ+ individuals have been in leadership roles within movements. This has expanded both the goals of movements and personal style statements—from gender-nonconforming outfits to powerful message T-shirts declaring things like "I can't breathe."

Beyond movements and making political points, Black people have embraced personal style as a form of public play and materialized imagination. Although not entirely disconnected from important freedom movements, there are powerful imaginative threads co-creating tangible representations of multiple sides of the self, articulated through attire.

Assigning value to them as not entirely separate from resistance but possessing value outside resistance is important. This thought brings me back to a powerful quote by adrienne maree brown: "I touch my own skin, and it tells me that before there was any harm, there was miracle." As politicized and violated as Black bodies may be within colonial structures, solely positioning them as battlegrounds for resistance erases their miracle as spirit-filled canvases for beauty and adornment. This erasure is not only reductive; it is its own violence.

–

DETROIT-BASED URBAN PLANNER Ritchie Harrison, whose parents were always elegantly dressed, had a weekend church ritual. "My brother and I always got fresh haircuts on the Saturday before church service, and I can still smell the Royal Crown hair oil intermingled with the hot comb used to straighten my sister's hair." All three siblings in the home had meticulously ironed outfits laid out on their beds for them. When they arrived at church, the trio was always asked about their grades and complimented on their appearance. There was an expectation that they would, according to Ritchie, "act and look good," in that order.

This was largely due to their grandma, Daisy, whom everyone described as "jazzy" and "stylish." She often wore sharp black-and-white outfits, which she rotated with purple pieces, as purple was her favourite colour. Grandma Daisy accessorized with matching silver jewellery, especially stacked bracelets.

Back before any of the grandkids were born, Grandma Daisy suffered a great loss. In 1966, Harold, her husband, died suddenly, and she was left to independently raise Ritchie's mom, then sixteen years old, and her two younger siblings. During that time of grief, Grandma Daisy ensured that she and all her children looked presentable in public. "My grandmother always said that your clothes don't have to be new or fancy, but they can look good." Continuing to dress well wasn't Grandma Daisy's superficial attempt to cover up their family's pain. It was her way of adding a bit of sweetness and dignity to their daily lives as the family carried the weight of their loss in public spaces.

Today, Grandma Daisy lives with dementia and is cared for full-time by Ritchie's mom and aunt. As Grandma Daisy approaches her 101st birthday, the sisters continue to ensure that their mother is stylishly dressed as a reciprocal act of love and preservation of her dignity.

Unlike Ritchie, whose family arrived during the Great Migration, his partner Clarinda's immediate family moved to Detroit during the 1980s. Also an urban planner, her fashion cues came from her three older siblings' preoccupation with not sounding or appearing *country*. Her brother Alfred was especially bold, oftentimes dressing in Run-DMC-inspired track pants and Adidas running shoes. Clarinda keenly noted how he and her other siblings cultivated personal style as a pathway into the big city and coveted peer groups. "Observing this as a young child gave me the permission I needed to boldly use fashion to self-express when I became a young woman," she says.

Clarinda characterizes her coming of age a decade later as an unabashed showcase of Black pageantry. "The entire community was a runway—parks, streets, and the mall were an opportunity to joyfully showcase our sense of style."

Ritchie chimes in, recalling how young Black men would cruise the mall wearing crisp polo shirts with a French tuck, before French tucks were a thing. They did it their way: "Our shirts hung loose and flowed with our slightly exaggerated stride, complemented by a matching pair of Air Force Ones."

These uniforms worn by young men created a fashion fraternity, acknowledged by subtle nods on escalators and in the food courts. "The way we publicly expressed ourselves through style was not just about simple consumerism," Ritchie says. "It was a way of celebrating and participating in our culture."

Clarinda underscores the importance of this type of joyful cultural participation by revisiting the exquisite style of Detroit's first African American mayor: "Take, for example, Coleman Young. Many white people at that time criticized him for his flashy fashion sense, but it was more than that."

Coleman Young's family closed down their dry-cleaning business in Alabama, where he was born, and relocated to Detroit during the Great Migration. Like many young Black men at the time, he worked for the Ford Motor Company. During World War II, he honourably served with the renowned Tuskegee Airmen, and he was arrested with fellow servicemen for insisting on the freedom they fought for at a segregated base near Seymour, Indiana. Before he was mayor, Young knew his self-worth and wasn't shy about wearing it on his back.

He was a handsome man who wore exquisite suits with perfectly placed pocket squares. Sometimes he swapped out a matching blazer for a slick velvet jacket or fur coat. The stripes on his suits and shirts were different colours and sizes but always complemented each other, and his hats topped off already great outfits.

As with most politicians, his policies and compromises are debated, but few debate the positive impact of Young's unabashed swagger. "Witnessing Mayor Coleman's style was really uplifting because it suggested that as Black Detroiters, we could be creative and self-express everywhere, including spaces unintended for us," recalls Clarinda.

Young's example has influenced both Clarinda's and Ritchie's professional aesthetics as they navigate senior roles. In 2023, during a trip to Accra—a Ghanaian city lauded as one of Africa's fashion capitals—Clarinda travelled to the studios of talented local designers. When she came upon a contemporary-cut suit constructed out of a gorgeous gold-and-purple printed African fabric, Clarinda immediately said, "I'm going to wear this to the office."

Although antithetical to so-called responsible greys and calming corporate blues—the uniform of Western workplaces—Clarinda felt a sense of joy and agency wearing her newly acquired suit while carrying out her professional duties. Her suit, and perhaps the confidence with which she wore it, elicited curiosity about its cultural origins. Clarinda proudly answered each question; however, she wasn't seeking validation. "I didn't need anyone to understand or affirm my choice to wear an African-inspired purple-and-gold suit with big swirly patterns to work," she says.

But the thing is, she received it—affirmation, I mean. Younger Black women thanked her for wearing that suit to work. Something as simple as wearing a suit rooted in her ancestral culture, constructed with exuberant fabric and woven with regal continental gold, granted her younger colleagues permission to present themselves in ways that felt good to them. Just as Mayor Young inspired Clarinda to express her personal style within professional spaces, she was modelling this for a whole new generation of young Black professionals.

Ritchie feels strongly that this type of bold attire is at once inspirational, shaping urban fashion trends everywhere, and unfairly critiqued. "Black people are often diminished as being label-obsessed or financially irresponsible for self-expressing through fashion, but this assessment is misguided." He explains that our personal style is not strictly about vulgar consumerism or financial illiteracy. "Even if there wasn't a single designer brand or a store to purchase trendy items,

Black people throughout the globe would find a way to dye something a bright colour and make a headpiece from found objects," he explains.

Notwithstanding the fact that Black people, like other oppressed groups, feel the pressure to prove our worth through costly clothing, there is indeed something in our cultural DNA that gravitates toward bling and bold colours as celebration, outside capitalism.

Not only is this bold self-expression ancestral, according to Clarinda, it is tied to our sense of self-actualization, which she describes as "a tangible and creative expression of prosperity, whatever that means for each individual, or a tangible and creative expression of an aspiration."

She also points out that it is a way of honouring community. When she and Ritchie get ready to go out, whether to meet a friend for dinner or to support a local event, they dress themselves in a way that makes them feel fly as a couple. They are also conveying to their community "that they are worth the effort," explains Clarinda.

Far from frivolous and more than resistance, Black people's style has always represented our materialized imaginations and shared cultural vernacular. It's one of the ways we've waged and won joy on our miraculous bodies.

-

SEVENTEEN OR SO years ago, back when Chase Cantrell was still a young lawyer working with major firms, he was negotiating multimillion-dollar real estate transactions on a daily basis. But something felt amiss. Despite Detroit having a Black population of about 85 percent at that time, none of the deals Cantrell was working on included Black developers. That is, until an older colleague, Larry, and a group of partners invested in a big retail development project on the city's edge, at Woodward and 8 Mile. "One day," says Chase, "he pulled me aside in the corridor and told me that he really admired the work I was doing."

The compliment came with a challenge. During the brief exchange in the corridor, Chase's colleague encouraged him to see himself on the other side of those big real estate deals. "After commending me on my work, Larry said, 'As good as you are at your job, you don't want to be the attorney on the deal forever.'" The conversation, which lasted all of five minutes, inspired Chase to take his legal training along with his adeptness for fostering relationships outside the institution and into the community.

Amid the spread of speculation—the practice of purchasing underdeveloped land or properties anticipating significant increase in value—and Detroit's "comeback" narrative, Chase realized that Black people needed to quickly regain ownership of places that had been ripped out from underneath them during the city's infamous 2013 bankruptcy. In 2016, he founded Building Community Value—an organization that provides technical assistance to would-be Black developers—as a way of ensuring that the city's future included the very people whose lifeblood had in large part shaped its character. His organization creates access to resources—in terms of capital knowledge and networks typically held by white developers—so that Black and other racialized individuals and nonprofits can play a role in tangibly shaping spaces in their city.

Initially, the organization was strictly focused on residential housing, with the goal of rebuilding the foundation of Black homeownership. This work indirectly correlated with maintaining a sense of presence in public spaces like streets, parks, and markets, which Black residents have informally stewarded and animated for decades. However, as Building Community Value grew, so did the development interests of his participants.

This, in large part, may be because Detroiters, like other individuals living in Black-majority cities, have a history of successfully creating spaces for themselves. With a critical mass of people and greater combined capital power, the possibility and perhaps sense of responsibility are greater than when Black people reside in places with relatively small numbers.

When speaking about this sense of responsibility, Chase metaphorically takes me into the archives. Over the past several years, he has been doing genealogy research and learned that his great-great-grandfather Simon Patterson was the president of what is reported to be America's first "negro fair."

Founded by three African American men in 1867 as part of the Sumner County Colored Agricultural Fair Association, the event was formally referred to as the Gallatin Colored Fair. Attractions included baseball games, a Ferris wheel, and a merry-go-round. People dressed up in their Sunday best to enjoy these attractions along with horse shows and musical performances.

It is striking that just a couple of years after the Civil War, Black people sought to not only build economic and political power after centuries of unfathomable oppression; they also prioritized the development of joyful places. Consider how important public joy must be to our community if a group of formerly enslaved individuals, relishing their still newly achieved freedom, came together to build a fair.

The original site, now surrounded by a worn seven-foot-high fence and the type of striking disparity common in North American cities, wasn't exactly what Chase hoped for when he set out for Tennessee to retrace his great-grandfather's footsteps: "Through the rusted chain-link fence, I could see unkempt grass and dirt, not much more." The surrounding neighbourhood was a mix of new condo developments and low-income housing. "Thankfully, I'd read a lot about the fair prior to my visit so I was able to activate my imagination to recreate what once was, but it was really difficult amid so much erasure." Even the plaque commemorating the site was a half mile away, which troubled Chase. "There's a very real history of Black people proactively creating spaces for joy and then having those places disappeared by the state, white mobs, or market forces."

While Chase's visit to the site evoked mixed feelings rather than joy, it helped him to make sense of his passion: "It's kind of like when an artist finds out that someone in their lineage was also creative . . . I felt connected and like I make sense."

Back home in Detroit, Chase continued to contemplate the erasure of Black spaces, which is a prescient concern as the city is experiencing a reverse exodus of sorts while welcoming new residents and businesses. Growth is a natural part of cities, but Chase fears that spaces that have historically centred Black public joy are at risk: "Plazas like Hart located downtown, the African World Festival, the Jazz Festival . . . so many spaces and events where Black people felt relatively safe to express joy have become costly or are overly policed or [have] disappeared."

He pauses to mourn the closing of the Woodward, Detroit's oldest gay bar, which burned down on June 14, 2022. As a blissfully married gay man, Chase is committed to the preservation of public spaces that hold multiple parts of Black people's identities. "In cities like Washington and Atlanta, a lot of gay bars like the Woodward are closing, and while these bars may not be Black-owned, they are important spaces that foster joy for Black 2SLGBTQ+ communities." Overall, he laments that there are fewer and fewer places where Black people can "go and laugh loud, express vulnerability through free-flowing tears, break out into a spontaneous hustle . . . smoke weed if that's their thing."

I smile at his reference to the spontaneous hustle. Once, on the last day of teaching a placemaking class at the University of Detroit Mercy's School of Architecture and Community Development, I found myself in the hallway with a handful of students committed to teaching me the hustle. Apparently, the hustle is serious business in Detroit, and there are several variations, each dedicated to a particular musical artist or song. I'm not sure which one I was messing up that day, but I'll never forget how exuberant I felt when that university hallway transformed into a dance floor. I viscerally understand why many legacy Detroiters are so concerned about losing spaces that foster Black public joy.

–

HAVING GROWN UP in Jamaica, an island where people greet each other with "everything irie?"—a patois phrase for "everything good?"—Carl Cassell was used to a warmth, beyond the temperature, which permeated public spaces. At home, Carl navigated markets and riverbanks with an ease and confidence that left him entirely unprepared for the chilly reception he would receive when the plane touched down in his country of choice.

Upon completing studies in economics and math at the University of the West Indies, Carl immigrated from Jamaica to Canada. Arriving amid a recession in the early 1990s, he traded in hopes of landing a job as an economist or even an entry-level banking position for an apron in the back of a restaurant. "One moment I thought I was headed towards a career in finance and the next I found myself three feet deep in a dirty pot," he says. His professional circumstance was worsened by the way he was treated when he untied his wet apron with wrinkly fingers and ventured out into the city.

His presence on streets and in shopping malls was often perceived as an intrusion or threat. When searching the eyes of pedestrians to approach and ask for directions, he became invisible. The latter issue—not being seen—was the most difficult part of Carl's early experience, largely because of his birthplace.

Carl hails from Cockpit Country, which is Jamaica's largest contiguous rainforest and is underlain by an extensive network of limestone-rich caves. Beyond its beauty, the place is revered for its history. It is where the Maroons, an indomitable group of enslaved people who fought and fled to the highlands, formed independent communities centuries ago. Carl and his family are direct descendants of these fierce freedom fighters.

His knowledge of his ancestral lineage instilled within him a powerful pride of place and personhood. "Where I come from, when we encounter people in public, we respectfully acknowledge their presence, and we expect the same in return." The small rural community is also where he developed an appreciation for public joy. His father, Hugh, owned a shop that sold everything from animal feed to Avon cosmetics. Every year, he would thank the community for its patronage by throwing a street dance in the square.

For a community of fewer than five hundred families, this was a momentous annual occasion. The sound of the truck travelling over rugged roads with gigantic sound systems ignited anticipation among country folk of all ages. A goat was killed to be curried and eaten alongside white rice, coleslaw, and fried plantain. Its head and belly were used to make mannish water, an aphrodisiac soup said to increase the virility of men.

Ska and reggae blasted from the speakers and DJs engaged the audience in call and answer refrains. Lovers leaned up against the speakers, slowly gyrating to slower tracks. Children like Carl, granted a reprieve from regular bedtimes, were permitted for one night to party with *big people* and snuck sips of beer left over in bottles. This core childhood memory is still vivid for Carl: "There's something about watching my people so elated that they literally danced off their shoes."

Carl had a natural penchant for the green spaces here in Toronto. He started spending a significant amount of time at Trinity Bellwoods Park, where he encountered a convergence of the city's social clusters. Wading through skinheads, Portuguese kids with pit bulls, and undercover cops reeking of Hugo Boss cologne and wearing New Balance runners, Carl found refuge among young men whose hands made space for them.

He felt a kinship with these new friends—from plumbers to visual artists—of all races involved in the city's hip hop scene. Bonded by their love of music, the small group gathered in the park most evenings after work to debrief their days, sometimes veering off into personal relationships and politics. "To be honest, we were mostly meeting up to smoke some weed in peace; we weren't solving political problems," he says.

Being in the company of people who made things reminded him of his boyhood in the mountains. From an early age, he had explored the arts, from painting to woodcarving. He and his childhood friends even made their own chisels by heating large nails in charcoal and then flattening them with a hammer. Hanging in the park reminded Carl that he was a man who knew how to create things, and so he got to work doing just that.

Over the next five years, he pursued and successfully attained a degree in commerce. During study breaks and the long commute between home and school, he made art with found objects, drawing inspiration from the city's cultural scene. Although he now held two degrees, Carl was unwilling to be at the mercy of the economy or limiting ideas about where he belonged. "I realized that if I wanted to achieve my dream in this country, I'd have to literally build it with my own two hands, not pursue it in places that didn't welcome me." He took a bartending job at night and during the day, his friends from the park taught him everything from plumbing to drywall to painting. He began to apply his newly acquired skills in the building where he lived. He helped update units in the building, and his landlord gave him a break on rent.

Growing up, Carl had spent summers on his grandmother's farm in a parish called St. Elizabeth. Linette Roy cooked massive pots of savoury and spicy dishes for her farm workers. Carl paid close attention to how to prep meat and fish and how to intuitively measure the precise amount of fresh herbs and coconut milk when preparing Jamaican dishes. He was also entrusted with a special job: "I was my grandmother's firekeeper; my job was to gather wood and stir up the embers to keep three fires beneath three massive pots going throughout the day."

All of this experience culminated in a search to find a space in Toronto to house his dreams. The first couple of months were discouraging. Landlords were not particularly eager to rent to a young Black man aspiring to open a hybrid restaurant and cultural hub.

After a string of refusals, he entered a space that the locals colloquially called "the crack bar" and made the owner an offer. With a foot already out the door of the derelict business, the owner quickly accepted.

During the first week, while cleaning the bathrooms, Carl realized how brittle the bones of the space were. He regretted his decision. But there wasn't a path leading backwards. A neighbour helped him install the exhaust hood in what would become his first up-to-code professional kitchen.

Standing in his newly constructed kitchen, Carl was grateful to his grandmother for teaching him how to cook and keep the fires aglow.

In mid-April 2001, Irie Food Joint opened its doors. Its motto was "Food. Music. Art. Culture." This distinct recipe for public joy guided its design.

"I am an artist first and foremost and so I'm very sensitive to spatial arrangements and the creative practice of welcoming," Carl says. Many Jamaican homesteads and public spaces have clear sightlines to land, water, and mountains. Because of the tropical climate and communal culture, the connection between internal and external spaces is an implicit part of the island's design vernacular. Upon entering Carl's restaurant, patrons had sightlines to the open kitchen and outside onto the patio.

Carl hung his own artwork and the work of local artists on the walls. Alongside this carefully curated collection, he displayed what we would refer to as crocus bags, which are reusable jute bags that Jamaican women use for carrying their fresh fish, ackee, yams, and other foodstuffs from the market. The juxtaposition of these bags alongside fine art was Carl's way of visually elevating the worthiness in the beautiful simplicity of Jamaican culture.

A collection of mid-century modern chairs and heavy wooden tables anchored the space. This mixture of luxe and sturdy furniture was intentional. Carl wanted de man 'dem to be able to bang dominos on the tables and audiophiles to jump out of their seats when taken over by the spirit of live music. He wanted aunties to bring their hot sauce from home as long as they were open to taste-testing his. "The space needed to be well designed but also accessible and sturdy enough to withstand our bombastic cultural expression," he says.

Carl also paid close attention to the pace of the space. It was important that it operated on Caribbean time. Unlike the typical restaurant practice of turning tables over as quickly as possible, Carl wanted people to feel like they could linger regardless of the size of their order or ability to extend a generous gratuity. "I wanted people to come for the food but stay for the slow and easy Jamaican vibe."

Carl's unconventional business model, prioritizing joyful placemaking over profits, paid off. Within five years, Irie Food Joint became a central gathering space for everyone who loved Black culture, regardless of identity. He gained respect as a restaurateur within the city's competitive gastronomy landscape—so much so that he earned enough social and financial capital to open a second location. Harlem, located near the city's Gay Village, would become a true community hub.

One afternoon, a DJ named Blackcat walked into Harlem and requested space for a regular ballroom night—an underground party featuring performances such as strutting, lip-synching, and audience engagement. These parties were established by Black queer and transgender individuals in multiple cities in response to public space laws prohibiting dressing outside gender norms and to the discrimination that racialized 2SLGBTQ+ individuals faced within mainstream queer spaces. Although Carl wasn't entirely familiar with the history and creative expression of ballroom, he was committed to creating a space that celebrated Black people of all identities.

Once, while working in the basement during the party, he heard several loud thuds. Rushing to the main floor to see if everyone was all right, he found ballroom performers voguing and doing acrobatic splits. Breaking into laughter, he was both relieved and honoured to co-host such an electrifying weekly event.

The programming of the space didn't always arise from formal collaborations. Sometimes the moment asked, and the space answered. For instance, in 2009 when Michael Jackson died, a graffiti artist felt inspired to create an art piece on the industrial-style garage door leading out to Carl's back patio. Patrons poured into Harlem, raw with grief. They were provided with markers, which they used to write messages around the spray-painted portrait. By the end of the night, everyone had laid down their grief on the dance floor and the garage door had become a memorial.

This became a ritual of sorts, repeated in 2013 when Nelson Mandela died, and again in 2016 when we lost Prince. On both of these occasions, the community came to collectively choreograph their grief. The door, now a living record layered with three portraits and hundreds of heartfelt messages, is a testament to the responsiveness of the space.

Another moment of historical significance was tied to the U.S. election in 2008. Carl purchased televisions, something he'd long resisted doing, wanting to minimize the distraction of screens. But with the possibility of the United States electing its first-ever African American president, he knew people would want to watch the coverage together.

As anticipated, community members from all ends of the city converged on Harlem. Their hope was so irrepressible it stretched itself across tables and hovered expectantly over the dance floor. It was as though the room had collectively inhaled—a singular contracted expansion filling the space.

When it was announced that Barack Obama had indeed been voted the first African American president of the United States, the DJ dug deep into the crates for celebratory tunes as heads turned toward the heavens. Amid the jubilation, Carl heard something that delights him to this day. All of the Black men in the space started addressing each other as "Mr. President." "They'd say, 'Why congratulations, Mr. President' or 'Good to see you out tonight, Mr. President.'"

The giddiness expressed by grown men, who are usually guarded in public spaces, was like nothing he'd witnessed before. It was the expression of a pure boyish joy during a moment when it felt like we could remake the world.

–

WHEN HE WAS a boy, Mitchell Silver's favourite green space was Brooklyn's Prospect Park. This 526-acre park is adjacent to the Brooklyn Museum, has numerous sports facilities, and boasts the borough's only lake. Back in the 1970s, most families like his didn't have access to such a grandiose green space.

In fact, the part of the park bordering Flatbush, an area in Brooklyn with a large Black population, was the only section without an entrance at that time. Still, Mitchell has many cherished memories of enjoyable outings to the park with his Haitian American mom, Jewish American father, and siblings. That is, until the helicopters came.

One evening while playing war—a game where children divide into teams and capture one another across predetermined territories—he, his brother, and a group of ten or so friends heard helicopters overhead. When cop cars followed, they became certain that they were the target and began to round each other up, hiding in the park berm and bushes.

In 2014, that same little boy would return to the site where his joy was disrupted—as the New York City Parks Commissioner.

The path toward that milestone wasn't without hardship. At twelve years old, Mitchell lost his mother, a head nurse and educator, to cancer. With her final breaths, she asked Mitchell to bring his tape recorder to the hospital, and she recorded a message. He labelled the cassette *Mommy* but didn't listen to it until several years later. Once a gifted runner and student, by that point, the weight of his unprocessed trauma had left him motionless. It was as though his mother had anticipated this crossroads. He listened to her message: "She implored all of us kids to get educated and make a difference in the world."

After completing his GED, Mitchell earned his bachelor's degree in architecture at the Pratt Institute, followed by a master's degree in urban planning at Hunter College. It was 1993, and he was thirty-three years old and quickly establishing himself as a visionary in urban planning circles.

In 2011, he was the first Black person elected president of the American Planning Association. He led the city-planning department in Raleigh, North Carolina. When he received the call to return to New York to head up one of the most remarkable park portfolios in North America, he hesitated. A Brooklyn kid to the bone, Mitchell had grown to also appreciate the livability and warmth in Raleigh. However, Mayor de Blasio dangled a carrot that led him back to the Big Apple—Mitchell would have the opportunity to not simply lead but transform New York City's park system.

Upon his return, Mitchell quickly established his priorities. Primarily, he wanted to ensure that all New Yorkers had equal opportunity to enjoy well-designed and well-maintained parks. "I watched the way stress fell off the shoulders of people like sweat as they entered Central Park, and I wanted that for every person in every park," he tells me. This meant paying more attention to communities that had been historically disadvantaged through divestment and inequitable park policies. Parks in these areas were often smaller, had fewer amenities, and had design features like spiked fences that diminished their beauty. Many of these communities are comprised of large Black and Brown populations. And so, he made a pointed effort to restore and create Black joy in numerous parks.

The healing process began by listening and observing. Mitchell observed Black families with members of all ages pouring into public parks at the first glorious sign of summer: "It was like a weekly homecoming; Black parkgoers would arrive early, finding shade beneath their favourite tree or planting a blanket before some type of body of water." Young children tickled their noses against flower petals and tested the prickliness of grass. Others squealed in a mix of fright and elation while swinging from the highest monkey bar or racing down the slide. Young women read or braided each other's hair on blankets. Beneath the bouncing ball, there was a constant negotiation of space and extension of praise. The aroma of dishes from across the diaspora always stimulated his senses. "My favourite part of witnessing Black people in parks was inhaling the scent of Southern barbecue or Jamaican jerk," he says. And, of course, there was music. Whether emanating from a boom box, a group of elders breaking into an old-time gospel verse, or the chorus of side-stitch-inducing laughter—with us, there is always music.

As part of his outreach, Mitchell laced up his running shoes and headed over to meet fifteen or so women, along with a small group of children, at Brownsville's Betsy Head Park. These were the members of We Run Brownsville, a running group conceived by two lifelong friends, Dionne (beautifully pronounced *Dee-own*) Grayman and Sheila Gordon. Following a brief yet warm welcome, he joined the group in a run. The first thing he noticed was the horrible and unsafe condition of the track.

Still, while dodging dangerous potholes and surface cracks, the women were having a great time. They ran at a pace where they could maintain friendly conversation in pairs and small groups of up to four people. The little ones headed for the sidelines after a lap or two but were clearly exhilarated to be participating. Following the run, Mitchell paused for photos and had the opportunity to hear the co-founders' stories.

Dionne was born in Brownsville and is part of the third generation of her family to live there. Although the community has the largest concentration of public housing in New York City, she didn't grow up in the projects. Her grandparents moved to a subsidized co-op community, representing a certain type of aspiration. Kids from the co-ops were expected to go to college or get a decent city job.

Sheila wasn't born in Brownsville, but her family's move to the co-op community where Dionne lived represented the same type of aspiration and came with the same expectations. She was twelve years old, and it was the first time her family didn't have to share a living space with relatives to get by. She recalls seeing Betsy Head Park back then, and although the weeds growing out of the track were almost as tall as she was, it didn't occur to her that she deserved anything better. She was a runner and grateful to have a place to run, even an unsafe, unmaintained place.

Dionne learned that Sheila, pet name Chee Chee, had moved into the 'hood through the preteen grapevine. Apparently, Chee Chee was dating Kevin. And not just any of the five Kevins in the crew at the time. Chee Chee was dating Kevin Lee, the coolest Kevin of all. "I had a platonic crush on Kevin because he was the funniest, most dope boy on our block," Dionne says. Dionne would find out who this new girl, who had swept in and scooped up the block's finest Kevin, was soon enough.

Denise Rhodes, a girl who wore tight Jordache jeans and four-inch heels, was having a sweet sixteen birthday party. Dionne and a select group of other twelve-year-olds were invited to attend. It was exhilarating being with Denise and the older kids, but the true highlight of the evening was when the DJ announced that Chee Chee was going to perform.

Dionne was intrigued. Chee Chee could also rap. How could this be? Dionne had never heard a female MC rap live before. A crowd quickly gathered around Chee Chee.

Throughout the decades, Dionne and Sheila rooted their sisterhood in a love for each other and their community. Brownsville, judged by stats, is a place of stigma and struggle. It is largely segregated, with a 76 percent Black population, and crime and chronic disease rates are concerningly high. But if you listen to the stories of residents like Dionne and Sheila, it becomes evident that Brownsville is beautiful.

It is a place with the most exhilarating pickup basketball games, producing stars like Fly Williams and Dwayne "Pearl" Washington. The neighbourhood has produced artists like BernNadette Stanis, who played Thelma Evans on *Good Times*, a groundbreaking 1970s CBS sitcom, and Yasiin Bey, formerly known as Mos Def, one of the most prolific, politically progressive rappers in history.

The community is known for its epic homecoming celebrations. These events , hosted across the United States, are often associated with historically Black colleges and universities. They uplift resilience, education, and joy. Brownsville homecoming celebrations pay tribute to the community's basketball legacy, emphasize the power of education, and are a platform for cultural expression.

As with many communities at the margins, Brownsville's poverty rate may be higher than the city's average, but its people are rich with creativity. And yes, Brownsville is tough, like Mike Tyson tough. The former heavyweight champion of the world grew up there and credits its streets for his resilience. That's not saying nothing. However, like Tyson, Brownsville contains intricate layers beneath its fierce exterior. In spite of its stats and scars, the community has multiple networks of care, and its people are compassionate and capable.

In 2015, Dionne, in a volunteer capacity, was vetting applications for health equity initiatives. She noticed that numerous corporations were vying for the small $10,000 pot of money. This was particularly disturbing because the funds were designated for community-led initiatives. Moreover, the application process was unnecessarily complicated. When a woman who ran a knitting group came to a meeting with her notebook and pencil to apply, she was asked extraneous questions pertaining to mission statements and budgeting. Dionne and Sheila took the woman aside after the meeting and helped her to write a successful application.

They did the same for another community member, which left $2,200 in the pot. Sheila suggested that, to respond to heightened health risks for Black women in Brownsville and beyond, they have a third party apply for this small amount of money to fund a running program primarily for Black women in the community. That is how they and the women they run with weekly got moving.

Their "active activism" mandate is rooted in evidence-based data pertaining to Black women's disproportionate health risks. A University of Boston article, citing numerous scholars who study how race, social structures, and neighbourhood environment impact health, found that "Black women are more likely than other racial and ethnic groups to die from cardiovascular disease, hypertension, stroke, lupus, and several cancers."

"The women we engage are literally running for their lives, but that doesn't mean that we don't centre joy in our group," Dionne says.

Rather than scaring women into running as a way of defying terrible health outcome odds, Sheila and Dionne centred joy as a key program principle. They invited participants to experience the serotonin rush of moving their bodies in the park while creating community. The pair strove to infuse their running program with the same joy, care, and unconditional acceptance of each other that they'd cultivated in their friendship.

Once, a participant arrived from work crying. She wasn't ready to talk about why, and joined the women for their run as planned. Afterwards, she felt ready to share that on her commute to the track, she learned that her estranged husband had cut her off his healthcare insurance. Immediately, numerous women in the group started offering resources and words of encouragement. "A lot of Black women are navigating difficult circumstances. They either leave their cares on the track or in the hands of their sisters," says Dionne.

Joy is also cultivated in the group through radical beauty. "The secret to public joy is that everything needs to be outrageously pretty . . . so much so that it draws people in," Sheila says. From ensuring that their water is adorned with beautiful fruit and edible flowers to providing women with vibrant T-shirts and socks for races, Sheila and Dionne pay close attention to how they present their program to the community. The pair joke that they attend races looking like they're outfitted for the Olympic Games. Ain't no raggedy runners or dowdy running gear on any of the sisters participating in this program. "If we see that a participant needs new gear, we will ensure that she gets it," says Sheila. This round-the-way relational approach permeates the group, reinforcing a sense of agency and mutual accountability.

But the one thing that these women could not fix on their own was the very track they were running on—the track that brought Mitchell to Brownsville.

On August 18, 2016, the City of New York announced that it would be launching the Anchor Parks initiative, a program conceived by Mitchell. With an allocated budget of $150 million, the program would carry out major improvements at five large parks. This was a bold approach because municipalities are annoyingly attracted to new, shiny things, which leaves low-income communities with aging and inferior infrastructure behind. Focusing on enhancing large existing parks was a way of asserting that the city hadn't given up on these places or, importantly, these people.

After seeing the conditions of the track at Betsy Head Park and striking up a mutual adoration with Dionne and Sheila, Mitchell was convinced that this particular transformation was an important municipal investment.

When auditing the park, Mitchell noticed that a huge concrete bandstand, including a massive wall, created a barrier between the park and street. He learned about the various sports, like softball, played in the park. This nuance, down to the renderings, was emblematic of the entire placemaking process. My favourite rendering, infused with goldenrod and fuchsia, depicts two young Black men chillin' on the grass. One of the young men is wearing an orange du-rag and balancing a toddler on his chest. It was evocative of a tenderness, an insider perspective that could only come from park planners with a genuine reverence for the community.

For Mitchell, the transformation of Betsy Head Park was a promise kept. There were new accessible entrances, adult exercise stations, and children's play spaces. There was an upgraded multi-use field where football, soccer, softball, and other sports could be played. Bleachers and informal seating were installed throughout. And, of course, the wonderful women of We Run Brownsville finally received a safe, resilient four-lane running track.

On the day of the ribbon cutting, everyone from the mayor to local residents was captivated by the park's transformation. The results shocked the hair on their arms to attention. This old, almost forgotten park now rivalled parks in affluent neighbourhoods.

However, the thing that brought many of the attendees, including Mitchell, Dionne, and Sheila, the most joy was what wasn't there. That big concrete wall had been removed. This made the park appear even larger than its already significant 10.55 acres. But more than that, its removal opened the park to the community. Residents could now witness the We Run Brownsville women's group doing laps around the track, children playing, and families bonding over outdoor activities. The new sightlines issued an invitation to witness and participate in public joy.

–

ONE OF MY most cherished photographs of my daughter was taken at her third birthday party. She is wearing red OshKosh corduroy overalls and a red turtleneck. Her hair is combed into two perfectly parted Afro puffs that look like ballons on top of her head. Strapped over her shoulder is a red-and-white keyboard-guitar instrument, which she is intently playing with a wild smile on her sweet little face. How I thought to coordinate her gift with her outfit, I don't know. What I'm certain of is that, even back then, I knew she was a star. Like a *star* star.

My daughter, Kirsten, an award-winning electronic DJ and producer, has already toured Europe more times than wealthy retirees take cruises. More than making and playing music, she is—in a way that is at once distinct but not entirely dissimilar from myself—a placemaker.

She started DJing a decade or so ago, shortly after dropping out of university. I recall the moment vividly. She was admitted to an undergraduate program the same year and at the very same university where I was admitted to a graduate program. I was delighted each time our paths crossed on campus. Her, not so much. As she walked away from one of our encounters, which I insisted on ending with a hug, I overheard her telling classmates, "That's my mom. No, I'm serious, that's my actual mom." I gave birth to her ten days prior to my twentieth birthday; the confusion and clarification were valid.

We spent the first ten years of my daughter's life, and my twenties, living in an intergenerational Jamaican family home. Her great-grandmother, whom she regards as her first friend, often picked her up from elementary school while I was working. Instead of watching after-school cartoons or soap operas, the pair prepared our traditional dishes together. Once, I arrived home to my grandmother teaching Kirsten and two of her classmates, no older than eight, how to fry snapper. I'm certain they'd hoped for cookies or pizza pockets. Instead, they found themselves in a kitchen with hot cooking oil crackling beneath the instructions of an old Jamaican woman intent on teaching them life skills. My daughter was, as always, beaming with delight under the tutelage and adoration of my grandmother.

Just over a decade later, those Caribbean cooking sessions with her great-grandmother would pay off. At the beginning of her DJing career, in addition to playing at local bars, she co-ordinated street parties, sometimes integrating recess games. In 2013, she launched a party called Jerk. Although she has always drawn extraordinarily diverse audiences, her Jerk party centres Black, often queer young adults. The name references a popular style of cooking, which fuses elements from indigenous Jamaican and African cuisines. Back then, she couldn't afford a caterer, so she prepared mounds of delicious jerk chicken herself. Integrating food into her signature rave was somewhat of an homage to those after-school cooking sessions. "The time I spent cooking with Mama is a nostalgic core memory for me," she says. "It felt instinctual to create an intimacy at Jerk by combining music and food."

The sense of intimacy she created, combined with her unparalleled ability to play what a cultural reporter and Polaris Prize juror referred to as "genre-obliterating" sets, made Jerk a well-loved rave within a few short years. When interviewed by *DJ Mag* about what had by then become a cultural phenomenon, she described Jerk as an ideal shared public space: "Like, what is the most ideal space? When do I think people are their best? What's the most fun thing that I like to do? When you make something like that, when you make a public space, it's not only yours, but it belongs to everybody. Jerk is something that belongs to me, and to the people who trust me to host it, and to Toronto."

Like all professionals who design and steward public spaces, Kirsten is focused on the cultivation of joy. For her, protecting these joyful spaces requires mutual agreement. "People take the labour required for curating good times for granted, but they are part of our social contract," she says. In the case of public parties and many other public gatherings, this social contract includes clauses about shared values and creating safer conditions—understanding that there are no wholly safe spaces. Also, clarifying how different bodies and creative expressions are going to be welcomed and valued within spaces is important.

When curating Jerk or performing at venues around the world, Kirsten considers barriers that may breach this social contract, obstructing everyone's joy. As a self-professed "seasoned partygoer," she's noted how mainstream public parties pride themselves on erecting barriers so that an abundance of joy is available only to a select few: "VIP lounges, rigid musical genres, and the performance of financial and social capital are all barriers limiting how much joy people are permitted to experience."

She credits raves—high-octane electronic dance parties embedded in an underground subculture that values bold artistic expression and social ideals—for dismantling many of these barriers, which tend to be steeped in class, commerce, and respectability. Because raves are primarily hosted outside conventional public party spaces, Kirsten is often presented with the possibility of empty industrial containers, which she designs from the floor to the exposed beams: "I've reconstructed rave spaces into enchanted forests using cherry blossoms and foliage, and other times used car parts to create a steampunk vibe."

And then there are what should be considered mundane details like free food stations with comfortable seating and ensuring that people of all genders can pee where they are most comfortable peeing.

Along with her space planning approach, Kirsten considers social aspects that either increase or diminish joy. She personally meets with security to ensure that there will be no policing of bodies or abuses of power. As with most raves, at her events, there's a general understanding that everyone belongs.

In more recent years, Kirsten has begun to consider what happens at her parties within a broader political and generational context. She's been thinking about the fact that her peers, Generation Y, are the first to be worse off than their parents. They are faced with a housing crisis with no end in sight and soaring education fees. Without revealing identities, she often tells me about acquaintances with degrees who sometimes have to resort to stealing groceries to survive.

I think about these issues through the lens of equitable urban development, and my daughter thinks about them through the lens of the public party. "When an entire generation is struggling to monetize their every interest or working three jobs to survive, dancing together becomes radical," she says. This is part of the reason there is no requirement to buy a new outfit or exclusive lounges setting people apart at her parties. This is also why she has donated party proceeds to numerous political causes and volunteers to teach young women how to DJ. "I didn't initially understand the magnitude of what I was doing, but now I have a deeper appreciation for the politics of the party and how there's a poverty of free time for my peers, so now I'm more able to go there fully—to be a part of the conversation," she says.

The thing that I most enjoy about her parties—yes, I'm a middle-aged lady at the rave—is how participatory they are. At first, it made me nervous, but I love the way hundreds of partygoers inevitably breach the boundaries of the stage within the first hour of her raves. She plays face to face, breath intermingling with partygoers, creating a visceral communal experience.

Oftentimes, there is a little elevated runway where self-selected featured dancers woo the crowd for hours on end, engaging with her as though they'd had a dress rehearsal. Sometimes the security guards begin to push people back, and in a polite yet authoritative voice that sounds much like my own, she always says, "No, let them through."

–

JOY, PUBLIC OR otherwise, Black or otherwise, is central to the human experience and cannot be simply summed up. Although there are clear and powerful similarities and tenets emerging from this work, as with every phenomenon, there are layers of nuance. Black public joy may look different across different Black cultures and geographies. Even within individual and regional Black cultures, factors such as sexual identity, class, ability, and gender interplay to either enable or diminish expressions of joy. Also, as online #blackjoy hashtags emerge, depicting folks frolicking on faraway beaches and checking out cultural spots, it's clear that some forms of public joy ain't cheap. And as I've learned over a half century, with the blessing of time and communion in community, we can find our way back to those childhood expressions of joy shamed and feared out of us.

This is my hope for every single human being.

Because Black public joy is no more or less important than any other form of public joy. All people are deserving of the promise of public spaces. We all yearn for the feeling of belonging, delight, and beauty as we navigate our daily lives. It is, however, important to acknowledge that some of us experience considerable unfairness, and sometimes unsafety, when it comes to accessing public joy. We cannot underestimate how the history of the auction block—a history we've all inherited—has resulted in public space policies and design adversely impacting Black people.

Despite this history and its impacts, Black public joy is not solely a Black concern.

Just as interdependence permeates public safety, the same is true of public joy. Regardless of our identities, the moment we leave our homes our access to and sense of joy become intertwined. Every gesture, from ceding space on a sidewalk to nodding your head to bombastic beats radiating from a street festival, influences the amount and quality of public joy available to ourselves and others. Every bus ride, trip to the bookstore, and coffee shop meetup presents us with the responsibility to be good stewards of each other's public joy.

With this awareness, we, all of us, arrive at a place where we must ask ourselves: How, on a daily basis, do I diminish or increase the joy of everyone I encounter in public?

In the case of Black people, this personal awareness and principle of stewardship is particularly salient because so many partake in and emulate our expressions of public joy. There are few people, particularly in major cities, who haven't dapped their friend as a greeting, borrowed a bit of swagger from our streetwear, or felt emboldened by the fierceness of our protests. This isn't to suggest that expressions of public joy are solely shaped by Black people. Public spaces expose us to many beautiful expressions of public joy and broader cultural influences. What I'm saying is that given that Black public joy has persisted through an egregious history to uplift our communities and many others, it behooves us to honour it—the people and the phenomenon.

Black public joy is rooted in an underexplored and unacknowledged cultural intellectualism. While unapologetically flashy, globally emulated, and ever-evolving, there is considerable thought beneath expressions of Black public joy. Understanding uneven power dynamics, so many of its expressions—such as mocking enslavers as part of a carnival or the raising of the Black Power salute at athletic medal ceremonies—were and are intentionally subversive, cloaked in celebration. Double entendres in hip hop lyrics reinforce humour and an insider cultural dialogue despite the genre going international. And when Keisha wears her extra-large hoop earrings to her administrative support job, know that she is not only joyfully asserting a cultural aesthetic, she is flipping off every stuffy institutional convention.

Our public expressions of joy—however playful or entertaining they may seem—are intentional, analytical, and acutely aware of our surroundings.

They have been perpetuated by a people who along with intergenerational trauma also possess intergenerational joy, an intergenerational joy that is in many ways inexplicable, given the ground upon which it was cultivated. A joy passed down from the enslaved to the emancipated through ritual, song, prayer, dance, food, and adornment. An intergenerational joy that is both embodied and a human right. An intergenerational joy that is intrinsic and soul-deep, reflective of our cultural character and not resisting anything outside of ourselves. And although parts of this intergenerational joy that has been passed down to us are too sacred for words, its alchemy and cultural intelligence do indeed have clear characteristics and curvature.

Black people be loud. I'm not suggesting that we are a monolithic group with identical ways of being or that there aren't plenty of introverted or reserved Black individuals. However, I can make a confident overarching statement based on plenty of scholarly and round-the-way evidence. Take the full-on dialogue between the actors on the screen and the audience in the seats on the opening night of a Black film. Black people will loudly chastise characters, sing along with the songs they recognize, and predict upcoming scenes. In most cultures, this type of participatory film watching would be considered poor public space etiquette or outright rude. For us, it's half the joy of being in the movie theatre together.

Congregants deliver half the sermon in Pentecostal churches and ballers erupt in praise for almost-impossible playground three-pointers like an NBA title is on the line. When rappers receive awards, they quite literally holler at the entire block that held them down. And we blast our favourite songs from mini boom boxes strapped onto our bikes because why wouldn't we share our favourite songs with the world?

Connected to these polyphonic reverberations, Black people's public expression of joy is a language expressed through our bodies. Take, for example, breakdancing battles originating on the streets of New York, where primarily Black and Latino dancers worked out their beefs or repped their blocks through awe-inspiring acrobatic moves like the head spin and the windmill. Another way our joy expresses itself as an embodied language is through gestures. The slight upturn of the head when passing a stranger on the street as a show of respect, snapping of fingers at poetry shows as applause, and the now universal dap.

Apparently, the body (gestures, aesthetics, and paralinguistics) constitutes approximately 80 percent of all communication. If embodied communication is positive, research shows a reduction of stress, increased self-worth, and better relationship building. Our body language is extraordinarily sophisticated, and, much like linguistics, it is composed of structures, syntax, and semantics to express our joy and solidarity. What if those of us descended from enslaved people never really "lost" our languages? What if we translated words into new embodied dialects and established discourse too advanced for simple alphabets?

Related to expressions of joy and solidarity is witnessing each other. Our elders sit out on their front porches presiding over the streets, reminding neighbourhood children, often overlooked in classrooms, to put forth their best efforts. We pour libations at places like auction block sites and cultural celebrations in honour of our enslaved ancestors and elders who've passed as a public testament to the value of their oftentimes undervalued lives.

And for those of us still here, we have a simple saying, "I see you," which, depending on tone and intonation, can mean:

"I understand your life is in danger so I'm going to film this interaction with the police."

"You did that, congratulations!"

"Your struggle and sacrifice are not going unnoticed."

"Damn, your fit is fly as f***."

"We're glad you're out and proud; no homophobic bullshit is going down on my watch."

In a world where we are either hyper-visible or invisible, acknowledging each other's existence in ways that are compassionate and humanizing is a culturally distinct tenet of our joy.

And perhaps, most profoundly, we do not require a permit or permission for our joy. Our rituals—stretching all the way across the Atlantic Ocean and those conceived on lands where we were held captive—have always been an echo in the earth's inner core. We rejoiced throughout centuries-long winters before ever seeing the crown of a single bud that we could call our own.

We do not require a permit or permission for our joy.

We have not waited for the fulfilment of empty promises before currying a goat and picking some greens to place upon our tables of thanksgiving and celebration. Our pots, even when there was nothing but scraps of pig's feet and chicken backs, have always boiled over with savoury and spicy herbs and the sweetness of brightly hued potatoes. Somehow, there was always enough for an unexpected guest or to fill an empty plastic margarine container to send home with a single mother.

We do not require a permit or permission for our joy.

When we were legally disallowed from frolicking in public swimming pools or enjoying a night out at the theatre, we built our own places for pleasure. We transformed abandoned sharecropper shacks and empty fields into juke joints with nothing more than our bodies, blues music, and a little bootleg liquor. Well before DIY spaces and pop-ups were popular, we sold poorly recorded videos and CDs inside barber shops that doubled as community hubs. Hairstylists, who had no regard for municipal bylaws requiring approval to run businesses out of their homes, gathered women in their kitchen-sink salons for good gossip and even better braids and flat-ironed bobs.

We do not require a permit or permission for our joy.

Many of our movements started around tables in church basements but we have never relied on a building or man's doctrine to summon divinity. We have stomped, strolled, and chanted on desecrated ground, insisting that it could once again be made whole and holy. Our hope in the unseen and faith in future generations were unshakeable without threats of fire and brimstone. Our reliance on a strength greater than our own human understanding has been imperative for our miraculous survival. We are ready with the answer even before hearing the call.

We do not require a permit or permission for our joy.

While justice may be deferred and our invitations to balls permanently delayed in the mail, we have always known that the time and place for joy is now. There has never been a need for a special occasion to drape ourselves in gold and wear the yellows and psychedelic pinks of Caribbean reefs. Far from perfectly designed parks and plazas, and on street corners without the charm of hipster twinkly lights, we have known that joy emanated from within us. The block party, the slow bicycle ride, and that subway dance that went viral was what it was.

Because we were there.

What would change if we viewed our public expressions of joy as more than resistance or response? For all humans, the most radical cultivation and expression of public joy is joy for joy's sake.

—Jay Pitter

ACKNOWLEDGEMENTS

To the Creator, the source and designer of all joyful places.

For my loves: Kirsten Azan (daughter), Greg Jun Guiang (life partner), Ensil Pitter (father), and Esther (dog).

For the culture.

I'd like to acknowledge the trust, time, and insights extended by my colleagues, community members, and a few close friends in sharing joyful place-based stories: Orlando Bailey, Carl Cassell, Clarinda Barnett-Harrison, Chase Cantrell, Sapphira Charles, Selma Elkhazin, Sheila Gordon,

Dionne (beautifully pronounced *Dee-own*) Grayman, Ritchie Harrison, Lauren Hood, Carmen Mayes, Chukwuwuikem (*Choo-kwoo-wee-khem*) Peter Nnamdi Vincent Opara, April Taylor, Isaiah Trickey, and Nathaniel Wallace.

An extra special acknowledgement to the elders—the real OGs—for entrusting me with their time and extensive knowledge:

My beloved friend and mentor Mitchell Silver, a foremost urbanist who served as the first-ever Black president of the American Planning Association and, recently, as the New York City Parks Commissioner, completing over 850 projects.

Ms. Minnijean Brown-Trickey, a member of the Little Rock Nine—a group of high school students who courageously integrated their high school following the historic Brown v. Board of Education decision—a social work scholar and renowned social justice freedom fighter.

Elder Mary Mitchell and Elder Luella Hardin Marshall, the knowledge keepers, healers, and respected elders of the Orange Mound community. Sincere appreciation for Professor L. Anders Sandberg—a foremost scholar and exceptional human being—for his early interest in and engagement with my ideas long before I established a bi-national practice or was published.

I'd also like to acknowledge early "listeners" of this work: Sherry Hugh, Sunjay Mathuria, Sofia Ramirez, Lisa Webster, Lance Flash, John Sivills, April Taylor, and Greg Guiang. Additionally, I am grateful for the rich conversations I had with Marsha Battle Philpot, a revered Detroit-based citizen historian and storyteller, Dawn Wilson-Clarke, Hip Hop Clown and Community Leader, and Tiffany Denise Brown, Architect and Executive Leader. Thank you to Dr. Garfield Hunter for his literature review support. As an author who also leads a practice, I'd like to thank a few of my valued colleagues: Ivi Lindau, for providing critically important supplementary research support; and Anthony Banks, for his expert early review and fact checking.

Appreciation for the Penguin Random House and McClelland & Stewart teams—most notably Jared Bland, former publisher of McClelland & Stewart, for taking the time to understand me, my values, and my practice and creating meaningful space for my contributions; Martha Kanya-Forstner, VP, Penguin Random House Canada, for generously extending the opportunity to write this book; and Haley Cullingham, Senior Editor, for her political and literary acuity and delightful curiosities, which enhanced the book writing process. Deep gratitude to artist and curator Kiké Otuije for the book's special limited edition poster. Also, many thanks to other team members who lent their expertise to the publishing of this book: Tonia Addison, Crissy Boylan, Dylan Browne, Bree Duwyn,

Sarah Howland, Kimberlee Kemp, Rebecca Rocillo, Lorissa Sengara, Stephanie Sinclair, Sid Watson, and Noelle Zitzer.

To every person, in every city, who actively contributes to creating, protecting, and sharing public joy.

SELECTED REFERENCES

PART ONE: PERFORMANCE

Davis, B. R. (2023). The politics of racial abjection. *Du Bois Review: Social Science Research on Race*, *20*(1), 143–162. https://doi.org/10.1017/S1742058X22000182

Marx, K. (2024). *Capital: Critique of political economy, volume 1* (P. Reitter, Trans.). Princeton University Press. (Original work published 1867)

Nast, H., & Pile, S. (Eds.). (1998). *Places through the body*. Routledge.

Scully, P., & Crais, C. (2008, April). Race and erasure: Sara Baartman and Hendrik Cesars in Cape Town and London. *Journal of British Studies*, *47*(2), 301–323. https://www.jstor.org/stable/25482758

Yancy, G. (2008). *Black bodies, white gazes: The continuing significance of race*. Rowman & Littlefield Publishers, Inc.

PART TWO: RESTRICTION

Andrews, K. (2020, November 26). Minnijean Brown-Trickey: The teenager who needed an armed guard to go to school. *The Guardian*. https://www.theguardian.com/society/2020/nov/26/minnijean-brown-trickey-little-rock-nine

Bailey, A. C. (2020, February 12). They sold human beings here. *The New York Times Magazine*. https://www.nytimes.com/interactive/2020/02/12/magazine/1619-project-slave-auction-sites.html

Goluboff, R. L. (2016). *Vagrant Nation*. Oxford University Press.

Government of Canada Publications. (n.d.). *Consolidation of Indian legislation. Volume II: Indian acts and amendments, 1868–1975*. https://publications.gc.ca/collections/collection_2017/aanc-inac/R5-158-2-1978-eng.pdf

Jacobs, J. (1992). *The death and life of great American cities*. Vintage Books. (Original work published 1961)

Kärrholm, M. (2005). Territorial complexity in public places—a study of territorial production at three squares in Lund. *Nordic Journal of Architectural Research*, *18*, 99–114.

Lefebvre, H. (1991). *The production of space* (D. Nicholson-Smith, Trans.). Blackwell. (Original work published 1974)

Loewen, J. W. (2006). *Sundown towns: A hidden dimension of American racism*. Touchstone.

McKittrick, K. (2011, October 14). On plantations, prisons, and a black sense of place. *Social & Cultural Geography*, *12*(8), 947–963. https://doi.org/10.1080/14649365.2011.624280

Nasheed, J. (2020, February 3). The 15th amendment was ratified more than 150 years ago, but the fight to protect Black voters continues. *Teen Vogue*. https://www.teenvogue.com/story/15th-amendment-ratified-150-years-ago-fight-for-black-voters-continues-og-history

National Archives. (n.d.). *Dawes Act (1887)*. https://www.archives.gov/milestone-documents/dawes-act

National Archives. (n.d.). *Executive order 10730: Desegregation of Central High School (1957)*. https://www.archives.gov/milestone-documents/executive-order-10730

University of Arkansas, University Libraries Digital Collections. (n.d.). *Gov. Orval Faubus declares a state of emergency*. https://digitalcollections.uark.edu/digital/collection/Civilrights/id/1254

Watson, H. (2000). *Narrative of Henry Watson, a fugitive slave* [electronic edition]. Academic Affairs Library, University of North Carolina at Chapel Hill. (Original work published 1848). https://docsouth.unc.edu/neh/watson/watson.html

PART THREE: PROTEST

Baron, Z. (2020, June 5). Jailed Ferguson protester Joshua Williams wants to be out there with everyone. *GQ*. https://www.gq.com/story/joshua-williams-ferguson-2020-interview

Bates, D. (2014, August 17). Mother of policeman who shot dead Michael Brown was 'a serial con artist who defrauded thousands of dollars from neighbors in stolen credit card scheme'. *Daily Mail*. https://www.dailymail.co.uk/news/article-2726614/Mother-policeman-shot-dead-Michael-Brown-serial-artist-defrauded-thousands-dollars-neighbors-stolen-credit-card-scheme.html

Calamur, K. (2014, November 25). *Ferguson documents: Officer Darren Wilson's testimony*. https://www.npr.org/sections/thetwo-way/2014/11/25/366519644/ferguson-docs-officer-darren-wilsons-testimony

CBC News. (2015, September 18). *Sisters recall the brutal last day of Oka crisis*. CBC/Radio-Canada. https://www.cbc.ca/radio/unreserved/reflections-of-oka-stories-of-the-mohawk-standoff-25-years-later-1.3232368/sisters-recall-the-brutal-last-day-of-oka-crisis-1.3234550

Cooper, B. (2018). *Eloquent rage: A black feminist discovers her superpower*. St. Martin's Press.

Duster, C. R. (2017, July 26). *Ferguson community center opens, once site of burned gas station*. NBC News. https://www.nbcnews.com/storyline/michael-brown-shooting/ferguson-community-center-opens-place-burned-gas-station-n786646

Eads, M. (2020, July 14). Years before Breonna Taylor's death, LMPD officer's Lexington supervisor saw issues. *Lexington Herald-Leader*. https://www.kentucky.com/news/local/counties/fayette-county/article244213297.html

Henderson, A. Y. (2019, August 15). *Film connects a physical barrier between Kinloch and Ferguson with the legacy of segregation*. St. Louis Public Radio. https://www.stlpr.org/arts/2019-08-15/film-connects-a-physical-barrier-between-kinloch-and-ferguson-with-the-legacy-of-segregation

Lee, T. (2014, August 21). *Ferguson has always been a 'bad city for black people'*. MSNBC. https://www.msnbc.com/msnbc/ferguson-kinloch-police-war-community-over-50-years-msna395956

Lowery, W. (2019, August 9). Dorian Johnson, witness to the Ferguson shooting, sticks by his story. *The Washington Post*. https://www.washingtonpost.com/national/dorian-johnson-witness-to-the-ferguson-shooting-sticks-by-his-story/2019/08/08/79ff3760-b77e-11e9-a091-6a96e67d9cce_story.html

McCoy, T. (2014, November 25). Darren Wilson explains why he killed Michael Brown. *The Washington Post*. https://www.washingtonpost.com/news/morning-mix/wp/2014/11/25/why-darren-wilson-said-he-killed-michael-brown/

McLaughlin, E. C. (2014, December 15). *Despite discrepancies, Dorian Johnson consistent in accounts of Brown shooting*. CNN. https://www.cnn.com/2014/12/14/justice/ferguson-dorian-johnson-statements

Melancon, T. (2018, February 9). The complicated history of race and Mardi Gras. *Black Perspectives.* https://www.aaihs.org/the-complicated-history-of-race-and-mardi-gras/

Robles, F., & Bosman, J. (2014, August 17). Autopsy shows Michael Brown was struck at least 6 times. *The New York Times.* https://www.nytimes.com/2014/08/18/us/michael-brown-autopsy-shows-he-was-shot-at-least-6-times.html?smid=pl-share

Schuessler, R. (2014, August 20). *Kinloch connection: Ferguson fueled by razing of historic black town.* Al Jazeera America.

Starr, B. (2015, April 17). *Missouri National Guard's term for Ferguson protesters: 'Enemy forces'.* CNN Politics. https://www.cnn.com/2015/04/17/politics/missouri-national-guard-ferguson-protesters/index.html

Timothy, R. K. (2018, May 3). Grief is a direct impact of racism: Eight ways to support yourself. *The Conversation.* https://theconversation.com/grief-is-a-direct-impact-of-racism-eight-ways-to-support-yourself-91750

U.S. Department of Justice. (2015, March 4). *Justice department announces findings of two civil rights investigations in Ferguson, Missouri.* https://www.justice.gov/archives/opa/pr/justice-department-announces-findings-two-civil-rights-investigations-ferguson-missouri

Williams, J. C., Holloway, T. D., & Ross, D. A. (2019, December 1). Witnessing modern America: Violence and racial trauma. *Biological Psychiatry*, *86*(11), E41–E42. https://pmc.ncbi.nlm.nih.gov/articles/PMC7220206/

PART FOUR: SACRED SPACE

Long, E. C. (1963, April). The placenta in lore and legend. *Bulletin of the Medical Library Association*, *51*(2), 233–241. https://pubmed.ncbi.nlm.nih.gov/16017286/

lovestoswatch. (2020, September 19). *Fixing a broken warp thread with very little yarn*. https://lovestoswatch.wordpress.com/2020/09/19/fixing-a-broken-warp-thread-with-very-little-yarn/

National Museum of African American History and Culture. (n.d.). *Symbols of black power in Vietnam*. https://nmaahc.si.edu/explore/stories/giving-dap

Puccini, M., & Horner, J. (2024, July 17). A short history of the rise, fall and return of Detroit's Michigan Central Station. *The Conversation*. https://theconversation.com/a-short-history-of-the-rise-fall-and-return-of-detroits-michigan-central-station-231566

U.S. Commission on Civil Rights. (2001, February). *Racial and ethnic tensions in American communities: Poverty, inequality, and discrimination volume VII: The Mississippi Delta report*. https://www.usccr.gov/files/pubs/msdelta/pref.htm

PART FIVE: JOY

Baldwin, J., & Stein, S. (2004). *Native sons*. Random House Publishing Group.

Donaldson, T. (2021, February 1). Dress and protest: Fashion hasn't been a bystander in the Black civil rights movement. *Women's Wear Daily*. https://wwd.com/fashion-news/fashion-features/feature/protest-fashion-black-civil-rights-black-panthers-blm-1234715312/

Emmons, R. A. (2019, December 4). Joy: An introduction to this special issue. *The Journal of Positive Psychology*, *15*(1), 1–4. https://doi.org/10.1080/17439760.2019.1685580

Gay, R. (2022). *Inciting joy: Essays*. Little, Brown and Company.

Martin, C. (2007, Winter). Remembering the Gallatin Fair. *Tennessee Historical Quarterly*, *66*(4), 370–373. https://www.jstor.org/stable/42628031?origin=JSTOR-pdf

Mudenyo, E. (2023, April 21). *NPM23 Blog: Pulling Joy Forward by Elizabeth Mudenyo*. League of Canadian Poets. https://poets.ca/npm23-elizabeth-mudenyo/

Palmer, L. (n.d.). With both hands: Poet Elizabeth Mudenyo. *Room Magazine*. https://roommagazine.com/whats-new/interview/with-both-hands-poet-elizabeth-mudenyo/

Tantum, B. (2024, August 13). Bambii: Beyond infinity. *DJ Mag*. https://djmag.com/features/bambii-beyond-infinity

Vinney, C. (2024, October 30). Experts reveal the one key difference between joy and happiness. *Verywell Mind*. https://www.verywellmind.com/joy-vs-happiness-8724682

READERS' GUIDE AND PUBLIC JOY INVITATIONS

Welcome, reader! This guide contains prompts for group discussion interspersed with invitations to explore the book's core concepts in actual public spaces. Also, as with the book, some of the questions and public joy invitations are universal and geared towards all readers, while others are directed towards Black readers specifically. In all instances, the intent is to encourage everyone to think more deeply about public spaces and the ways in which people of all identities can access more public joy and become better stewards of one another's public joy.

In keeping with author and placemaker Jay Pitter's approach, the goal is not only to encourage you to reflect and discuss—we also hope you will explore the book's concepts of public joy and experience the answers to questions we've asked in your own communities, bodies, and quiet reflection spaces.

Please note that while it's important to be candid as you work through the guide below, you are never obligated to share more information than you are comfortable with. Similarly, when participating in the public joy invitations, please engage in ways that are bold while keeping your comfort and safety in mind. Exercise your own good judgment, and check in with yourself as you participate in both discussion and action.

1. Let's kick off with words from the end of *Black Public Joy*. Towards the book's closing, Pitter repeatedly emphasizes: "We do not require a permit or permission for our joy." She also stresses that Black public joy does not wait for the "right" or "perfect" time to manifest: "We rejoiced throughout centuries-long winters before ever seeing the crown of a single bud that we could call our own . . . we have always known that the time and place for joy was now."

    - FOR BLACK READERS: When was a time that you publicly expressed joy despite not having a permit or permission to do so? How do Pitter's words resonate with your experiences of public joy, both personal and collective? Reflect on a time when you held public joy even if it didn't make sense. What was it that sustained your public joy during that difficult situation?

- **FOR ALL READERS:** What do these two quotes about public joy reveal about the Black community, and about other historically marginalized communities? Why do you think these are the words and ideas that Pitter chooses to emphasize at the end of the book? What do these words reveal about Pitter's definition of public joy, for the Black community and in general?

2. Pitter writes: "Spatial entitlement is a term I use to describe how social conditioning and uneven power relations mediate the quality of public space we feel we deserve, the amount of public space we take up, and the way we move through public space." What are some outward signs of healthy spatial entitlement that you've observed in public? It could be bold clothing, loud laughter, or a demand for accessibility. What about unhealthy spatial entitlement? It could be someone taking up space in ways that are unkind or inconsiderate of others—for example, manspreading on a crowded row of subway seats—or citizen profiling.

3. Though she didn't have the words for it as a kid, Pitter learned early on the politics of public performance, and how they combine with racial stereotypes to shape

and restrict Black people's freedom to just *be* in public. The next time you're out in public, on your way to work, school, or the grocery store, consider the way that someone's dress or tone of voice may be elements of a carefully calibrated performance.

- FOR BLACK READERS: Consider the spaces in which you feel a heightened pressure to perform "properly" in public, versus the spaces in which you feel emboldened and encouraged to embody and express yourself fully. How do these public spaces increase or reduce your opportunities for joyful expression?

- FOR ALL READERS: With honesty and curiosity, consider the ways in which you as an individual might have been socialized to unintentionally act as a surveillor of Black and other groups of people who've faced disproportionate public space harms. Take note of your judgments and knee-jerk reactions to moments when the performance of "normal" public behaviour is broken by someone refusing to adhere to the rules. What are the unconscious or conscious standards of public performance you may be holding that person to? Are these standards fair and/or kind?

4. Pitter writes: "To be under the gaze . . . is to have an awareness, which is sometimes anxious, of being looked at and judged by other individuals or groups . . . The gaze implies a power relationship between the superior 'gazer' and the inferior 'object' who is forced to perform and practise self-regulation when under surveillance." Reflect on a time when you found yourself under the gaze. What was it about the place you were in or the people you were with that created this sense? How did being under the gaze affect your engagement with that space and the people in it? On the flip side, reflect on a moment during which you were fully in your public joy without performing or orienting yourself towards the gaze—neither restricting yourself nor acting publicly joyful simply as a "f*ck you" to the gaze. What was *that* place (and/or the people in it) like? How did you find yourself engaging with it as a result?

PUBLIC JOY INVITATION: Now that we've identified the impacts of the gaze, how do we deal with it? Pitter shares her strategy: "I play prerecorded messages in my body . . . I remind myself that I belong wherever I am. I belong in public spaces that contribute to my health, opportunity, and sense of curiosity. I then tell myself that I'm attracting so much attention because of my swagger, striking features, fashionable outfit, and/or the vibrant energy I brought into the space." Write down and memorize your own public space message for resisting the gaze. The next time you are in a public space and feel like you are under a restrictive, judgmental gaze, recite your message to yourself. Believing your message may take a while, so be patient with yourself, and persist.

5. Consider Pitter's multifaceted approach to scoping out a public space, which goes beyond the usual urban planning logistics to include learning about the space's history and feeling her way through its connections to communities both present-day and ancestral. As she writes about her research: "These embodied experiences have exposed me to a vibe that transcends conventional urban planning conversations, veering into the poetry of place." What do you think is the importance of centring these ways of knowing and understanding a place, which engage not only the logical mind but also the human heart and spirit?

PUBLIC JOY INVITATION: In an increasingly digitized world, many of us are distracted and might often take the physical public spaces we pass through for granted. Put down this book and go for a walk/roll through a public space in your neighbourhood. Practise moving along your familiar pathways with new and curious eyes. What do you notice about the way these spaces are designed, and the way that you and the people you observe interact with them? Where is the public joy?

6. Pitter writes: "[P]ublic spaces tell us the truth about who we are, and serve as a litmus test to reveal the true state of our democracy and, importantly, our humanity." What do the public places in your community and/or city say about its values? Whose wellness and public joy do they prioritize?

7. Think about the land you live on, its Indigenous history, current Indigenous contributions to it, and your own history within it. What are your connections to this land? Whether you are Indigenous, or a newcomer, or descended from a long line of settlers, we all have land-based histories and joyful rituals. What are yours, whether individual or communal?

PUBLIC JOY INVITATION: Head on out to a cultural celebration taking place in your city, whether it's a powwow during Indigenous History Month or a Lunar New Year food festival. You can go alone or grab a friend! As often as you can during your time there, pause and observe the rituals and expressions of public joy happening around you, big and small. How does this community publicly manifest its joy? Do you see crossovers with your own community's rituals and expressions of public joy?

PUBLIC JOY INVITATION: Have fun at the cultural celebration you attended? Take it a step further and volunteer at another event geared towards public joy! As Pitter writes, we are stewards not only of space but of one another's public joy: "[We] all have a moral obligation to contribute to each other's sense of belonging." Afterwards, reflect on your experience. As a volunteer, what did you notice about the measures put in place by event organizers to ensure that all attendees were able to access public joy—not just safety, which as Pitter points out should be a given?

8. Let's take a look at Pitter's description of a photo of her grandmother with her two sisters on a Caribbean beach: "Their shoulders are squared off with the camera, not positioned sideways to conceal their bellies or create the illusion of thinner hips. All three women are concurrently occupying both places—their bodies and the beach." What does it mean to concurrently occupy both one's body and the place/space one's body is in? What are the places where you feel you're able to occupy both?

PUBLIC JOY INVITATION: Author and environmental activist Wendell Berry said: "There are no unsacred places; there are only sacred places and desecrated places." Pitter reflects "on how limiting the idea is that places of worship or pilgrimage routes are the only sacred sites." Do you and/or your community have a sacred public space? As soon as you can, go to that place and linger for half an hour. Take in the space with all of your senses. What are the qualities that imbue this space with sacredness?

9. When thinking about the violence of lynchings, Pitter remembers the words Southern urbanist Carmen Mays repeats to herself: "Black people and trees are sturdy and have the ability to heal from the harm." This leads Pitter to theorize that places, like human bodies, can be traumatized and desecrated by harmful acts—and can heal and grow beyond the violence. How does the body of a tree parallel that of a human or a community? Can you think of other parallels between human resilience and elements of nature or even human-made places?

PUBLIC JOY INVITATION: Pitter puts forward a radical reframing of marginalized bodies: "If war can be waged against Black and other exploited bodies, then what prevents those bodies from being reclaimed by individuals as sites for waging public joy?" What does it mean to wage public joy on one's own body?

- Think of two things you can do to consciously, intentionally wage public joy on your body this week. It can be anything from wearing a natural hairstyle or cultural clothing to dancing in the park to your favourite song to meditating in front of a body of water. Write these ideas down and do your best to put them into action. At the end of the week, check in with your body—what does it feel like to inhabit a self that you are making into a site of public joy?

PUBLIC JOY INVITATION: Throughout the book, Pitter emphasizes that Black people's public joy should be as much of a priority as their right to safety in public. Taking it even further, she argues: "There is a wealth of documentation focused on our public degradation; why not bend the narrative arc toward Black public joy?"

- FOR BLACK READERS: Think about the stories of Black public joy that bring your heart strength and healing. These narratives can be family anecdotes, memories made with friends, or stories you absorbed through social media, film, or books, whether fictional or non-fictional. Write these stories down in your own words, and dwell in the power they bring to your body.

- FOR ALL READERS: Consider how the news and social media often hyper-focuses on the Black community only during moments of pain and trauma, like during the protests and mourning that followed George Floyd's murder in 2020. What can you do to counter these dominant narratives with stories of Black public joy, artistry, and celebration? Research a story of Black public joy.

10. Many expressions of Black public joy have become universal in today's world. As Pitter writes: "There are few people, particularly in major cities, who haven't dapped their friend as a greeting, borrowed a bit of swagger from our streetwear, or felt emboldened by the fierceness of our protests."

- FOR BLACK READERS: What are the expressions of Black public joy and solidarity that generate a sense of pride and belonging within you? While many people who aren't Black might now use or practise those expressions, there will always be elements of them that remain Black people's alone. Reflect on what those non-transferable and precious elements are and take ownership of them.

- FOR ALL READERS: Take a moment to reflect on the public intellectualism of the Black community, and how its inspirations and influences manifest in your own community's expressions of solidarity and public joy. Do a little research into one aspect of Black culture that has become part of your own, be it a certain strand of music, dance, fashion, or other expression. What are the origins of that public joy–making practice in Black history, and at what point did it intertwine with your culture? Find ways to pay homage to the Black pioneers of this practice! For example, if it's a genre of music, seek out and share the music of the Black artists who were the first to create that music.

11. Pitter writes that Black people's inheritance is one not only of intergenerational trauma and pain, but of intergenerational public joy: "[a] joy passed down from the enslaved to the emancipated through ritual, song, prayer, dance, food, and adornment. An intergenerational joy that is both embodied and a human right." Let's pause on the notion of intergenerational public joy. What comes to mind for you? Also, consider the distinction between "embodied" and "human right." What do you think is the difference? What are the public joys that we all possess an inherent right to, no matter who or where we are?

Regardless of race or any other social category, every single person's public joy has survived something. Although our histories are distinct and personal experiences differ in how they have been subjected to systemic violence—like the auction block and the public space policies outlined in the book—it is important to honour the persistence of your public joy. Go out and demand a world that makes space for it.